C000089626

Edition 1.0

PUBLISHER'S NOTE

Every effort has been made to provide you with the latest, most accurate and up to date information possible at the time of publication, however, content may change without notice. Much of the information has been obtained through the personal experiences of the authors and ongoing feedback and research and is generic in nature and not specific to any nation's Defence Force in particular. Whilst the emphasis is of this book is directed at pilots, much of the information contained herein can be interpolated for Weapons Systems Operators (WSO), Air Combat Officers (ACO) and aircrew in general. This publication is not an official Defence Force document and is not intended for operational use. Original Defence Force operational documents are the source reference and authority. The authors wish to thank their respective Defence Force for the extensive flying training, operational and instructional experience received and all have no regrets about becoming Military pilots. Thanks also to Ronnie for the good times and everything in between.

Published by Blue Horizon Enterprises (BHE) Pty Ltd. Previous publications released by BHE:

Edition 1   "**How to be a RAAF Pilot**" April 2004 (Print and pdf format).

Edition 2   "**WINGS: How to become a Pilot in the RAAF. Edition 2.0**" published November 2005 (Print and pdf format).

Edition 3   "**WINGS: How to become a Pilot in the Australian Defence Force (ADF). Edition 3.0**" published January 2010 (E-book pdf format).

Written by Mal Bloggs, Esq
Copyright © 2015 Mal Bloggs and Blue Horizon Enterprises Pty Ltd. All rights reserved.
First Edition

ISBN 978-1-925128-82-6

electronic or mechanical methods, whether no known, or hereafter developed, without the express, prior written permission of the author, except for brief quotations contained in reviews and/or other commercial uses permitted under Australian and United States copyright laws.

For permission requests, feedback or errata, contact the author at bhorizonterprises@yahoo.com.au

Distributed as an electronic book by the Publisher.

Find us at **http://www.getyourwings.com.au**
Thank you for downloading our EBook. Please review this book on Itunes and Google Play. We need and value your feedback to make the next version better. Thank you and good luck.

Table of Contents

BLUE HORIZON ENTERPRISES
http://www.getyourwings.com.au

Preface

You start with a bag full of luck and an empty bag of experience. The trick is to fill the bag of experience before you empty the bag of luck.

~Old, bold pilot saying

Congratulations! You have purchased an EBook which gives you are rare insight into the inner workings of a Military pilot's course and how to become a Military pilot. How do we know this? Well, we were taught it, then learnt it through the experience of numerous squadron postings and then later delivered Military ground and airborne instruction over many years in single engine piston, advanced Military fast jet, tactical transport, rotary wing and turbo prop aircraft. This book is a condensed result of those personal experiences and is the only book of its kind based on real time military cockpit experience. It is riddled with a plethora of tips, techniques and actual cockpit transcriptions on how to maximize your chance to pass a Military pilot's course and become a military pilot. Once you get those WINGS or 'fun tickets', you will then be in for a very exciting life flying whatever aircraft your Military will offer you. They are all good, believe us. There is no such thing as a dud flying job.

WINGS: How to Become a Military Pilot, was written to:

- ✈ Assist you in obtaining entry as aircrew to a Military Service,
- ✈ Give you unique first hand guidance and tips on passing pilot's course,
- ✈ Provide personal insight into Military flying careers,
- ✈ Act as a one-stop-shop for individuals looking to become Military pilots, and
- ✈ Cater to students, civilian pilots and serving members alike.
- ✈ Describe the life of a Military pilot.
- ✈ Discuss the options available after your Military career.

Our EBook, **WINGS – How to Become a Military Pilot** is written by Military Qualified Flying Instructors (QFI) and gives you the real time critical information you will need to maximize your chance of being successful on the grueling but exciting pilot's course. We begin with a brief synopsis on the requirements for entry into Military service. We tell you what you need to know and how to ensure that you front up with all your ducks lined up. You will be completely ready for your formal Military application for service, but we don't stop there. Most of the information available up to this point is available through recruiting itself or online. This is what everyone else will have. As our loyal customer, we will then take you on a unique journey of what you will not be told. This is where you will gain a distinct advantage. For instance, it is important to also be prepared for pilot aptitude testing. The reason for this is that **when** you successfully meet entry requirements, you may be sent for aptitude testing quite quickly. We will dedicate a complete chapter to this specific form of assessment, which you can prepare for, before the event. We even have an app online for this express purpose.

After confirming your status as the pilot aptitude whip, it is now time to move to the really fun stuff, which is flying Military aircraft on pilot's course.

You have heard all of the stories, possibly even spoken to people who have done it. Now it's your turn. You will get one shot, so you need to make it count. It is really quite simple. Read this EBook and you will have a very good

chance at passing, which is no mean feat. It's a tough course, make no mistake about that. You will be challenged. A whim or a vague interest in flying will not sustain you on this course. You must have a burning desire to make it and a determined vision of yourself as a

Military pilot and leader in a Military environment. So saddle up for some damn hard work but by golly, it's worth it. Having those wings pinned on your chest will no doubt be one of the most satisfying personal achievements you have yet experienced. It is just the beginning of a career without equal. It truly is a life that is challenging, fascinating, exciting, and above all, rewarding. When you hear people say that it must be the best job in the world, they're right! Every Military pilot you ever meet will tell you that all **the hard work is worth it** and that **it is achievable!**

Sidenote

Whilst the information within this EBook is generic in nature and not specific to any nation's Defence Force in particular, the advice provided will be applicable to all forms of Military airborne instruction no matter which service or nation. Every effort has been made to provide you with the latest, most accurate and up to date information possible to arm you with the tools you will need to be very competitive at recruiting and on your pilot's course, no matter what service you choose.

The content of this book is based on extensive investigation of current recruitment practices, personal experiences and interviews with current applicants, student pilots and weapons systems operators and current Military pilots. Every attempt has been made to ensure the accuracy of the publication, however, with the passage of time, some of the information contained herein may change. Therefore the authors cannot guarantee the accuracy of the information and it should be remembered that this book is published as a guide only. The authors have tried, where available, to provide a reference, which gives the reader an opportunity to obtain the latest information available. We want to instill in you a desire to learn and to know more, so we will give you an opportunity to do so when we can.

During this book some of the terms are masculine such as airmanship and the use of the term he or his. Wherever the term his or her is used, it may be substituted for his/her. We have simplified the use of these terms to one gender at times to aid in document simplicity.

Our aim is to help you become a Military pilot. This book provides a plethora of anecdotes, war ries and personal experiences from numerous sources in Navy, Army, Airforce and Marines about about recruiting, training and life as a Military officer and pilot to better prepare you for a successful Military career. Paragraphs written in *italics* are actual events or thoughts from our own experiences. They are there to give you both personal insight into how we became Military pilots, and what we thought of the life in the Military at the time.

I had no family members in the Defence Force and I joined when there was no internet, so all the information was just word of mouth and brochures. The Air Force was actually better than I thought. At the age of 21 I had a University degree, a set of wings on my chest and I was jetting off to all parts of the world flying a VIP biz jet with some dollars in my pocket. Of course I worked really hard, especially in those first few years where there was a tangible risk of failure but the rewards were worth it and I have no regrets. I made some great friends that I still have today more than 25 years later. I would do it again if I could and I would encourage my kids to have a go if they wanted to. It's a good thing.

ABOUT THE AUTHORS

Blue Horizon Enterprises Pty Ltd consists of Military pilots all who are still flying, with a combined Military service experience of some 80 years and 25000 hours of Military aircraft flying experience. This consists of significant operational squadron experience including transport (VIP Jets, Heavy Military

Tactical and Strategic platforms), fast jet (Operational and Trainer) and rotary wing operations as well as extensive exposure to Defence Force recruiting and aircrew and officer training. All authors are Military Qualified Flying Instructors (QFI)with experience on basic, advanced and lead-in fighter airborne instruction. Between us, we have had postings as QFI, executives and Directing Staff at all levels of Military flying and ground training including Military Academies including Air Force Demonstration Formation Aerobatic Teams. Collective experience also includes ground based instructional postings to Defence Force recruiting, Ground Instructor and Supervisory positions at officer training facilities and the Defence Force Military Academies. We don't show photos of ourselves or even disclose our names. But we are real people and we have done this stuff for some time now and there is no substitute for years of cockpit experience and there is nowhere else on earth that you will find the stuff we are about to tell you in the one place. We wish you the best in your endeavours and hope that we have gone some way to help you in your dream to take up one of the most rewarding jobs in the world today. Good luck and fly safe!

CHAPTER 1

How to Prepare for Pilot Recruiting

You will be questioned extensively about various topics when you apply to join the Military. The key is to know what those topics are and how to answer those questions. We can help you with this. Blue Horizon Enterprises have spent a great deal of time helping future pilots get their chance to attempt a Military pilot's course. This is our fourth book on this topic. Our latest Ebook, **WINGS – How to Become an ADF Pilot** was written for Australian hopefuls looking for a crack as a pilot in the Australian Military. We have sold thousands of copies of our books and our pilot aptitude app with great feedback and success. Just getting onto a Military pilot's course is an achievement in itself and should not be underestimated. The more information that you have, then the higher your chances.

Your first step is to contact recruiting to receive a general information kit. Ideally this should be done about a year before your intended entry date. This kit will contain the minimum Military entry requirements and how to find out more information. There will be many factors to think about. You will need to consider each one of them carefully before you go into recruiting to formally apply as a Military pilot. Here is a list of those factors and we will discuss them briefly now for you.

SERIOUS BUSINESS

Flying Military aircraft is not all about leather jackets, fast jets and the movie Top Gun. It is serious and expensive business. You are about to enrol to be

9

trained for war and you may be ordered to pull the trigger and you may be shot at. This is no joke and you are possibly signing on to accept a large degree of responsibility in expensive, technologically advanced Military hardware on potentially a daily basis protecting your country and its citizens. In addition, you may be called upon to deploy at short notice into a warzone in a foreign country for no set timeframe. Know what you are getting in to.

OFFICER FIRST

You are actually joining the Military to become a leader and an officer first with a sub specialization of pilot, WSO or ACO. Hence, you will be required to undergo some form of officer and leadership training before starting a Military pilot's course. You will be expected to lead men and women and to set the example. So you will be assessed at recruiting as to your suitability and aptitude to become a Military leader. Are you honest? Do you have evidence of previous good judgement or the ability to prioritize and process information quickly and accurately? Can you make the right decision under pressure? Have you led before, if so, where and what was the outcome? Be prepared to answer questions of this nature at some stage.

EDUCATIONAL ACHIEVEMENTS

You don't have to have straight A levels although it would be handy! Normally you will not be considered unless you have satisfactorily completed at least year 12 academic studies. You need to know in about year 10 what subjects are acceptable if you want to be a pilot. There is no point rocking up with an A in basket weaving or tiddlywinks at recruiting on day one and being told that you are ineligible to become a pilot. You need to find out which subjects are compulsory. It varies from nation to nation but it is usually some form of Mathematics, science based subject and a high level of English. Remember it is not necessarily the actual grade that you get, but what percentage of your capacity was used to get it. For example, if you loafed along and received a few A's, they would much rather pick a candidate who worked their backside off and received straight B's. They want a candidate who has a proven record of working diligently and achieving results – an honest hard worker.

MEDICAL AND PHYSICAL FITNESS

There are a strict set of medical and physical fitness guidelines that are mandatory for entry into the Military. These are published and fairly easy to  obtain and will be listed to some degree within your information pack. The minimum entry standards are in place for a good reason. Once employed by the Military, normally your medical and dental will be free, so they don't want people with chronic ongoing issues that the Military will have to absorb at their cost. There are also certain medical conditions that are not compatible with Military aviation such as heart murmurs, asthma and color blindness to name a few. You will also be required to be a certain physical size and weight to get through the rigorous Military training and to fit into the various cockpits, which we can say are not always designed for comfort! You could be operating at high temperature in cramped conditions, under high G forces for extended periods. This can be taxing, believe us. You will also be asked many personal medical related questions and will undergo a pre-entry fitness test before being accepted. Previous use of hard-core drugs for instance, is something that they will find out and is something that should be disclosed early on. Normally this would not entitle entry into the Military. Find out the details well before applying formally.

CITIZENSHIP REQUIREMENTS

Generally only permanent citizens of your nation can apply or those who have formally applied to become one. This is a fairly easy question to answer but must be checked early in the process as it could be a show-stopper if you are a new arrival in the country for example.

11

SECURITY REQUIREMENTS

Along the lines of the previous paragraph, you will be asked quite a few questions about your previous places of residence, job history if you have any, associations that you are or have been affiliated with. For instance they don't want ex members of Outlaw Motorcycle Gangs, criminal enterprises or members who were dishonorably discharged from other Military organizations. They may also ask if you have had any previous security clearances and to what level.

AGE REQUIREMENTS

As mentioned earlier, you may be going to war, so they want mature individuals. Normally, the minimum age is 17-18, so that a graduate pilot will be at least 18. The Military are about to invest a lot of money in you and they prefer young and medically fit candidates. Generations of pilots have shown that the sharpest recruits come from the 17-27 year old age group. Again check with your recruiting for finer details.

SPEECH

You must have speech that is clear from impediments. This is due predominately to the obvious requirement to be able to speak succinctly and accurately whilst on the radio and to your subordinates

GENDER RESTRICTIONS

Many western air forces up until just recently, prohibited females from front line fighter aircraft. This has now effectively changed. Whilst the USA has many female fighter pilots, Pakistan has just had their first and the same with the UK. Here is one of them:
http://www.standard.co.uk/lifestyle/top-girls--the-women-patrolling-the-sky-for-the-raf-6385146.html

As yet Australia has no female fighter pilots. They have numerous female Air Combat Officers (ACO) who crew fast jets, but no pilots as yet. So if you are female, have a go – you could be the first or one of the very few in your country.

UNRESTRICTED SERVICE

You need to prove that you can serve anywhere on planet earth at short notice for possibly an unknown duration. So if you need access to some form of restrictive medication, have religion based restrictions or are dependent upon something that precludes this, then this may be a barrier of entry. If you think that you may be affected then contact recruiting to discuss further.

RETURN OF SERVICE OBLIGATIONS (ROSO)

If successful at recruiting and officer training, then you will be given a shot at pilot's course. Now it's hard work and exciting and all that, but the point is, training pilots is a super expensive business. For example, from zero to fully-fledged fighter pilot is easily around $10 Million USD. Just to pass pilot's course is approximately $500 000 USD or more just for an individual. Even candidates who do not pass, can cost hundreds of thousands of dollars. This doesn't include your salary, free medical and subsidized housing etc. So naturally, the Military are very thorough in their recruitment and testing in order to get the best candidate and they will want a return on their investment. They don't want you leaving after say two years post-wings to join an airline for instance. The Military normally obtain this commitment by ensuring that if successful on pilot's course that you will be 'locked in' for a commitment of time. Normally this is about 10 years post graduation but varies from country to country. There are severe financial penalties for leaving early! Remember, if successful, day one in the Military may be day one of possibly a 12 year commitment.

It is worth knowing this commitment and thinking about it carefully before signing into the Military. You should ask the question: Do I have to serve the ROSO if I fail pilot's course? In other words, if I do not pass and they offer me Air Combat Officer, Administration, Engineering, Intelligence Officer, etc, then am I required to remain in the Military until that ROSO commitment is complete?

It is worth noting that even as a pilot, not all of your 10 years or so may be in a flying post. You may be posted to ground jobs that needs pilots to fill them, such as being involved in aviation safety investigations for example. So you need to be prepared that you may have to drive a 'Mahogany Bomber' or desk for a couple of years, so find out what the details of the commitment that you are signing on for! Remember, there are always more bums than cockpit seats in every Military, so not every pilot flies all the time. In addition, new pilots are graduating every year trying to take your flying job in the finite world of Military cockpit available positions!

EX-MILITARY OR IN SERVICE APPLICATIONS

Many applications to become a pilot come from in-service applicants doing other jobs such as aviation technicians, sailors, Military police dog handlers or infantry soldiers for example. If they have a proven track record of achievement, are medically suitable and are well recommended by their Commanding Officer, then they may be accepted for pilot aptitude testing. Likewise you may have applicants who have flown for other nation's Military. Many are quite experienced and they may be eligible to be 'laterally recruited' perhaps even obtain their wings automatically depending upon the nature of their proven experience. This would all be negotiated at recruiting and would be subject to the Military vacancy rates, policies at the time and would be subject to a formal airborne validation course.

ENTRY OPTIONS

You will need some form of officer and general Military education and etiquette training. Find out what options are available, as you will be asked what you know about it and what your preference is. It is important to present yourself as someone who

knows this and is prepared to not only accept it but look forward to it. For instance, do they offer direct entry officer training (normally a 3 month course or so) and then perhaps straight onto pilot's course. Perhaps you may be able to join a Military Academy whereby you will study a tertiary degree first (and get paid for it!) and then begin your pilot training. This could be a 4 year degree before you manage to sit inside a cockpit. Another option is that the Military could sponsor you through a civilian University or College and then you start formal Military training on graduation. This is often enacted if the applicant has already had a successful year or two of University or College in the appropriate subjects and meets recruitment entry standards. Find out the options, where they are located and which one suits you. Here's one: http://www.defencejobs.gov.au/education/Adfa/

OFFICER TRAINING

Before formally applying as a pilot, you will be trained to become a Military officer. The details of the officer training options are beyond the scope of this book. A fairly typical and detailed explanation of Military officer training options is contained in our book **WINGS – HOW TO BECOME AN ADF PILOT** available on our website at http://www.getyourwings.com.au

It is also fairly easy to search online for the officer training options that exist in your country as many of the officer training facilities want you to join, so they will publish large amounts of data about what the course entails. Where is it? How long does it last for? What skills will you need before starting? What will you need to bring with you? What activities will you do? Get a copy of the Joining Instructions from Military recruiting. Here is a brief description of what your typical officer training will entail:

Initially, it will be a shock to the system, as you will be expected to do a lot of new tasks seemingly under constant time pressure. These tasks may seem menial and unrelated to flying such as ironing your own shirts, polishing boots and yes, potentially cleaning toilets! The Military use various terms to describe these tasks such as 'panics, bogging or rounds' depending upon which branch of the Military you are in. However, it is also a test of your motivation. Be ready for some hardship whilst undergoing officer training. It is not a joke. The weak will be found out. You will be constantly short of sleep. You will have restricted time off, possibly none for the first few weeks. You will be doing a lot of drill (marching), running, obstacle courses and generally challenging physical activities. You will be handling real weapons. You will probably go into the field and be navigating at night and conducting practical leadership exercises, often in groups. You will have endless inspections which often have to be repeated, as the standard is high. Eventually you will learn to be a leader and you will need to set the example without being told to. So lap it up. Get involved, stay focused on your goal, work together and smile. Be seen as a ray of sunshine.

It is important to remember that perhaps you could be surrounded by people who are also trying to be officers, but did not join as aircrew. For instance you could be in a group where you are the only pilot candidate and others could be training to be a Legal officer, Intelligence Expert, Engineering, Air Traffic Control, etc. The best way you can cope is to be known as a quiet achiever and to remain 'grey'. This means to not stand out too much. Don't be a bossy know it all (the brash shoot from the hip, John Wayne) but also don't be a meek mouse. Just fit in, get on with it and don't brag. This is a means to an end and remember they are trying to sort out the wheat from the chaff, which means strong versus weak candidates. It is not a competition as the Military are big enough to fit you all in. They want you all to pass. So be a team player. Help others even if it slows you down at times. If you are mature, hard working, honest and smile at least occasionally, you will be ok. Don't forget this fact: a very seasoned set of recruiting professionals have decided that you have the potential to pass, so have confidence, believe in yourself and be a team player. Some people really find out their limitations on a course like this, sometime for the first time in their lives. You will complete the course knowing more about yourself when you finish. Remember, these will be great times and you will make some great lifelong friends.

A fact worth remembering is that many candidates may have come from a very complimentary world. For example, they may have held a prefect position at school, been an academic high achiever, performed well in sports or music, just received their drivers licence, been successful at Military recruiting – so their life is full of compliments and well dones. Officer training may be the first time where you may get yelled at and where criticism can come from all directions. So don't be easily offended, listen to all advice and get on with the task. Your 'trainers' are just doing their job. Be ready to be tick skinned and get tough. Harassment is another issue and will not be tolerated within the Military. The Military have very clear procedures to deal with this issue in the unlikely event that it occurs.

Officer training doesn't last forever and this is why you need a strong desire to become a pilot as you will need to focus whilst undergoing your officer training to reach you ultimate goal - that is a chance on a Military pilot's course.

COMBAT SURVIVAL

At some stage in your training you will need to do an aviation related combat survival course. This is normally a mandatory requirement in order to become a Military pilot in the unfortunate event that you crash or are shot down as this maybe over enemy territory. You will be expected to be trained in the priorities of survival in various terrains from desert, water, jungle and possibly snowfields. You will be expected to live off the land and undergo extensive escape and evasion training as well as interrogation technique training. You will go without food on this course for a longer period that you will have done before. They want to see how you perform and think logically under such conditions. Also you will have no idea of the finer details of course content or duration as they want to simulate the uncertainty of being downed aircrew. Again they want to see how you cope with this uncertainty. Be ready for it and remember it's just another test of your motivation and desire. You will also be learning lifelong skills at the same time. You can now start to see that you must have a very strong desire to become a Military pilot as you have to not only pass various courses to start pilot's course but you need to thrive not just survive.

AVIATION MEDICINE

You will be extensively examined not only by a general practioner doctor, but also by a qualified aviation medicine expert. It's not rocket science, but the Military need to know that you are fit and healthy to operate potentially some of the highest performing, most technologically advanced equipment on planet earth. Additionally, service in the any Defence Force requires particular personal qualities, a high level of physical fitness and freedom from some disabilities and ailments that may seem insignificant in civilian life. This is especially the case for pilots for obvious reasons. Unlike civilian employees, members of the Military are required to carry out a wide range of arduous Military duties (often in isolated and stressful circumstances) as well as the duties within their specialised role. In an operational area or a war zone there are no guarantees that anything other than the most basic medical care and first aid will be available. Consequently, medical and physical standards for entry into the Military are high and applicants who have medical conditions, which prevent them from offering unrestricted operational service, cannot be selected for enlistment. These high standards are set not just for the benefit of the Defence Force, but also to protect you and your future health and to avoid problems with any existing medical condition that may be aggravated by intense physical activities or exposure to the airborne environment. Consequently, you will require an examination of: ENT (Ear, Nose, Throat), Cardiology (Heart), Audiology (Hearing) testing as well and an extensive series of eye tests by an Ophthalmologist to mention a few. This will be all paid for by the Military and everyone who wants to be an pilot has to do it. Discuss any personal potential shortcomings in this area with recruiting as they may well have faced a similar problem before.

WORK EXPERIENCE

Recruiting may ask a question like, "So you want to be a Military pilot, ok, how do we know that you didn't think of this yesterday? What evidence can you provide us with to prove that this is a long held interest of yours?' It would be great to say something like: 'Well I saved some money and paid for my own flying lessons and went solo'. Another response could be: 'I found out about your scheme to offer aircrew applicants a chance to spend a week with an operational Squadron and I took up this opportunity.' Not only will this look good at the time, but think of all the real time information that you will have obtained by speaking to those who are living the dream. And it's free. Find out if this option exists in your area, as it is most worthwhile. It also separates you from the crowd as most will not do this, or even know about this.

Another question they may ask is if you were a Military cadet in your youth. Again this is proof of a long-term desire to become a Military pilot. Whilst not essential, this would be good to have done. You can now hopefully see how you would become more attractive to the Military if you had accomplished just some of these tasks compared with a person who had never read this book and just walks in off the street. Here is an example of a typical Military program: http://www.defence.gov.au/workexperience/

PREVIOUS FLYING EXPERIENCE

We at Blue Horizon Enterprises often get asked whether previous civilian flying experience is an advantage and whether you should undertake it before applying to be a Military pilot. Military flying training and subsequent Military operations are quite different to any form civilian flying. Whilst perhaps an indicator of innate motivation, we have found that civilian flying experience does not necessarily increase performance pilot's course.

Decades of statistics and also our personal exposure to teaching experienced civilian pilots versus students with no previous flying experience, has confirmed this affirmation. Indeed, some applicants have found it difficult to adapt to Military techniques as a consequence of their previous experience. This could be due in part to applicants who have significant experience and reinforcement of different techniques to those used in Military aviation. For instance the only way to fly straight and level by day in the Military is by ensuring you carry out the Attitude - Lookout - Attitude - Performance (ALAP) work-cycle. Civilian pilots may have never heard of this and may be reliant on autopilot, or something different. This would have to be unlearnt.

Others have found their previous civilian experience helpful in other ways. There have been many cadets or students with significant flying experience who have attempted pilot's course. This level of experience has ranged from a one hour introductory flight to having over 3000 hours of flying experience as a qualified airline pilot. No matter how much civilian flying experience a candidate has, the nature of Military flying and the content of the syllabus will challenge all candidates at some stage. Remember you will be conducting flying exercises that are not done regularly or even at all in the civilian flying world – for example; close formation (flying within 2-3 metres of another aircraft at 500 kph, or faster), low level navigation at 250 feet at 500 kph or faster and aiming to find a precise target within 15 seconds after 100 minutes flying time, for example. Civilian pilots do not get exposed to this sort of flying.

Accuracy standards are very high for good reason. For instance, bombs need to be dropped at precisely the right place and the exact time required or there could be friendly personnel still in the area. If you fly too high at low level, then you could be detected by radar and shot down. Flying too low at high speed and you could hit the ground in a moment of distraction. We call this "Head in Shed = Dead". Near enough is not good enough for the Military. This is one of the biggest phase shifts that you will face coming from the civilian flying world. You must always strive to be 100% accurate and perform the 'perfect' sortie or mission although obviously this is not always possible for many reasons. For instance, the Military ideally want speed control at all times to be +/- 5 knots and altitude to be +/- 50 feet. Height errors whilst at 600 knots at 150 feet above the ground can have disastrous consequences. Sustained errors outside of Military accuracy standards can show a lack of mental capacity, fixation and limitations in potential.

There may be an opportunity in civilian flying to develop habit patterns not necessarily beneficial to Military aviation. For instance, in the Military, many aircraft require that the checklist be recalled flawlessly from memory alone, especially emergency procedures in single seat aircraft. The Military checklist is simply a backup if required. Many civilian checklists are read out and are challenge and response style. Pilot's course students must operate independently utilizing memorized procedures without errors often under time constraints. In this case, it may be easier to teach an aviation novice new habits from the beginning rather than convert or unlearn some habit patterns attained by a high time civilian pilots who undergo pilot's course. Having said this, many high time civilian pilots do quite well especially early on in the conversion phase, due simply to their exposure to the airborne environment, but this slight advantage fades quickly.

No matter who you are though, you will have to work hard, particularly after hours, to possess the required knowledge to pass pilot's course. All approved applicants, regardless of previous flying experience, will attempt a full pilot's course, i.e, there is no Recognition of Prior Learning (RPL). The nature and content of your civilian flying experience will be assessed if and when you are required to undertake flight screening, but more about that later. So in summary, whilst usually no harm is done having flown civilian aircraft, it does not construe any real tangible advantage overall on pilot's course performance.

PUTTING IT ALL TOGETHER

Each topic covered in this chapter should be examined in detail before formally applying to enter the recruitment process. This is a fairly obvious statement, but you would be amazed how many people apply to become a Military pilot and don't know the first thing about the Military they intend to join. So ideally if possible, try to start maybe a year or two before making an official enquiry. Remember, you will be examined on your level of knowledge about what you are about to possibly devote at least 12 years of your life to (more in some cases). They will also probe your motivation for wanting to become a Military pilot. You should go to your local library and perhaps read a couple of books about the Military you intend to join. Another useful source of information is the respective service website. For those applicants intending to apply for the Australian Defence Force (ADF), you are in luck. Check out our website: http://www.getyourwings.com.au

This website has useful, relevant online content including personal videos, photos, online aptitude testing sample questions as well as useful downloads. It also has our latest Ebook:

WINGS – How to Become a Pilot in the ADF.

Whilst this EBook specifically targets entry into the Australian Military, it is a good read for anyone wanting to join any Military as most pilot selection processes follow a very similar process.

Hopefully, now you can see that by attending to the details that we have touched on this chapter, you will be miles ahead of a candidate who just walks in off the street hoping to get to first base in becoming a

Military pilot. You are off to a great start. Knowledge is power. You are now somewhat educated about what you are about to apply for. You are hopefully strongly motivated and you have some evidence of past performance. Already 60% of the candidates will not follow you to the next phase. So now you have the information you need to formally apply for Military pilot. Your next step is to start preparing for pilot aptitude testing, which could happen fairly quickly **WHEN** you are successful at applying for entry as a pilot. In the next chapter, we will prepare you for pilot aptitude testing.

CHAPTER 2
Military Pilot Aptitude Testing

irstly let's emphasize and summarize the last chapter to ensure you get to pilot aptitude testing day. You will be faced with various challenges when you apply. In reality, the first step is really quite simple. Try to go into recruiting a year or so **before** you intend to apply if at all possible. Most people will be eligible, but to stand out from the crowd, you will need to prepare **before** you formally apply. So to summarize chapter one and to enhance your chance of becoming one of the 40% or so who pass it through initial assessment day, make sure that you address the following issues by doing the following:

✈ **Desire**   Make sure that becoming a Military pilot is really what you want to do, it's serious business. Believe us, you must be committed to make it.

✈ **Leadership**   You will be required to lead. Try to provide examples of you having successfully done so.

✈ **Academic Subjects**   Make sure that you are doing the correct, applicable subjects otherwise you could be wasting your time applying.

✈ **Academic Subjects**   Make sure that you are doing the correct, applicable subjects otherwise you could be

23

wasting your time applying.

✈ **Academic Ability**   Just do the best that you can, as these results will be analyzed.

✈ **Medical Fitness**   If you have any issues, find out what they are and sort them if you can before applying, ie are you color blind for instance? You can do a colorblind test online. Remember you will be medically examined probably in more detail than you ever have before.

✈ **Dental Fitness**   If you have any issues, find out what they are and sort them if you can before applying. Don't show up requiring 3 molar extractions!

✈ **Citizenship**   Are you a citizen of the country whose Military you intend to join? If not, apply to become one before applying for the job.

✈ **Security**   If you have any dodgy affiliations sever them now. Be able to account for the places you have lived and perhaps the countries you have visited over the last 10 years. Don't try to hide anything as they will probably know more than you do!

✈ **Age**   Are you within the required age limits?

✈ **Speech**   Is it clear and free from impediment?

✈ **Gender**   Does your country allow pilots of both genders?

✈ **Unrestricted Service**   Make sure you are prepared to serve anywhere at any time. Can you prove it?

✈ **ROSO**   Are you prepared to serve the stipulated minimum period, Can you prove it?

✈ **Officer Training**   What do you know about what could be in store for you? What are the options available? What is your preference? What does the course entail?

✈ **Combat Survival**   Where is it located and what do you know about it?

✈ **Work Experience**   It would be good here if you could provide some evidence of previous aviation interest: undertaking your own flying or enrolling to visit a Military base if that program is available. Were you a Military cadet at some stage? Stand out by proving that the statement "I have always wanted to be a pilot" is true for you, as everybody says it but not everybody can prove it.

When you can answer these questions, it will be obvious to the Military recruiting agency that you are genuine. They will see that you have bothered to find out the requirements and then you have addressed them individually to ensure compliance. This will not go unnoticed.

So ok, you are ready to contact recruiting and formally apply to become a Military pilot. Now here is a hot tip that will place you ahead of your peers. **You need to ensure that you are prepared for pilot aptitude testing before you formally apply to the Military to be a pilot.** Why do you ask? If you are a great candidate (which this book will help you become one), there is a chance that you may be placed into the next available slot on pilot aptitude assessment day once your application to join has been successfully processed. This could happen very quickly and could perhaps be within a week or so. This is not the time to start preparing for it! So much of what we are about to tell you here, should be attempted **before** attending this assessment day. You can always 'brush up' your knowledge as you get closer to the actual pilot aptitude assessment. Anyway more about pilot aptitude testing in a moment. For now let's focus on how to ensure that you get there but first a quick mention of waivers.

WAIVERS

Under certain circumstances, candidates who do not meet all the entry requirements may be considered for a waiver and allowed entry into the Military, but the candidate must offer a distinct and tangible benefit to warrant waiver considerations. The following are tangibles that may be waivered:

Age, education, NMUD, character, medical, psychological testing results, undischarged bankruptcy, citizenship and checkable background requirements, but there are caveats and restrictions here.

APPLICATION DAY

So now you are formally ready to apply. You know that you meet the minimum entry standards. You now send in the application paperwork which will include personal particulars, an extensive medical questionnaire and various questions on achievements in sport, academics, committee's and employment if any. Your application has been examined and you receive a letter back inviting you to attend a formal application day at recruiting. Travel to and  from recruiting is normally required to be paid for by the member. Travel to and from the various agencies you may be required to attend such as medical institutions and flight-screening facilities are normally aid for by the military.

This application day is a 'two arms and two legs check'. So first impressions count. This is where the recruiting staff get a chance to see you in person and get to match the face with the voice and the application paperwork. As soon as you walk in the door to apply for the first time, the assessment of you as a candidate begins. Do you have tattoos on your face or are you wearing an orange Mohawk? Don't be the one legged man trying to get a job as Tarzan! Ensure you are well groomed (no ridiculous long hair or earrings if you are male for instance) and **be on time.**

It is probably best to wear a suit or at least a shirt and tie as a minimum. For ladies, dress conservatively and look sharp. Remember you are dressing to one day set the example for others. All personnel involved in the recruiting process including civilians will be tasked with judging you as a Military pilot and officer candidate no matter what the rank of the person that you see. Don't be fake and try to impress, just be yourself and let your appearance and words do the rest. The application day is designed to give you a chance to demonstrate your inherent desire to be a Military pilot and an officer in the Military. It is also your opportunity to ask questions, so have a few good ones ready to go.

On application day, you will be required to bring personal documents including your birth certificate, photographic identification and evidence of educational achievements and the like. They may have further questions regarding your completed medical questionnaire and personal particulars form. Basically, they are searching for evidence that you meet the minimum entry criteria not just relying on what you have stated on the application paperwork. They are also looking at citizenship details, noteworthy medical issues and, of course, your achievements so far (scholastic, sporting or previous employment history). They are already evaluating whether you have the appropriate qualifications, medical clearances and required achievement levels to become an officer in the Defence Force and whether you warrant further processing. They do this via a tick sheet. You may also chat with a recruiting officer who may ask you some basic questions about the topics listed in the previous chapter. Make it easy for them by ensuring that you have attended to all of the items. You may also receive preliminary medical screening usually done by a nurse. They will look at height, weight (due to ejection seat limits), pulse, basic eye test and possibly take ergonomic measurements of seated height, (buttock to knee and buttock to heel lengths) etc to ensure that all of your parameters are within acceptable cockpit limits.

FITNESS TEST

All applicants normally will have to pass some form of Pre-Entry Fitness Test (PFT) before entry. This could be done on your application day or at another time but you will be advised in advance to make sure that you are ready. Typical tests involve a run of nominally 2-3 km, followed by maybe some shuttle runs, situps and maybe even some pullups. Find out the details early so that you can prepare for it.

Sometime after application day (normally within 2 weeks) the recruiting centre should contact you regarding the status of your application. Some people will only get this far. Don't be disheartened. If you really want it, wait a couple of months and then try again. They can then see that you are motivated if this is your third attempt! If you are successful, then you will be booked to join others on an aircrew aptitude assessment day. This assessment day is specifically for aircrew applicants and the actual date will depend upon when they have enough applicants to conduct one. For instance, they often have more assessment days near the end of the year as people are leaving school at that time and they will have more applicants to process. It could be anything from 7 days to a few months before you receive a letter informing the date of the next stage of the Military pilot recruiting process. This is quite normal.

So well done, let's assume that you have met all Military entry requirements and you are considered as an acceptable candidate to attend pilot aptitude assessment. You will get a letter inviting you to Military pilot testing. Nice work, so far. This is where the assessment of you as a candidate starts to cost the Military money, so they only send candidates there that not only meet the minimum entry criteria, but are presentable, well motivated and speak well. Basically, trained recruiting professionals think that you have a chance of passing the next step. Naturally, you will have followed our advice and have already done some targeted Military pilot aptitude practice. Now we will detail to you how to shine at pilot aptitude testing. You are off to a good start. The journey continues.

SPECIFIC MILITARY PILOT APTITUDE TESTING

When you are successful at the fact finding day, you will be booked in to attend Assessment day. The day consists of:

- ✈ Aircrew pilot Specific Aptitude Testing,
- ✈ More detailed medical assessment,
- ✈ Psychological interview, and
- ✈ Formal Defence Interview.

The Military pilot assessment day will generally start with a review of your entry data by an administration clerk and then you will sit down and speak to a formal recruiter. They will ask you some very basic questions like why are you here, when did you want to be a pilot, why should we pick you, what do you know about the day ahead, etc. Then you will head off for your formal aircrew testing.

Aircrew applicants will be asked to complete a series of tests to determine their aptitude and compatibility to become an pilot in the Military. Each nation is different, but in general it will involve mathematics, verbal and non verbal reasoning (testing your ability to think logically and clearly under time pressure), comprehension, vocabulary, interpretation of instruments, spatial orientation of aircraft in 3 dimensions and often a coordination exercise involving your arms and legs manipulating a machine. The aptitude/ability testing does exactly that: it tests an applicant's aptitude for aviation, general knowledge, IQ, logical thinking processes and underlying aviation related abilities. These tests are notoriously difficult to study for, and are really an indication of natural abilities. However, exposure to the sorts of questions that you could be asked before you attend this testing, will give you a distinct advantage. **You are in luck** as we will help you with some basic preparation on the types of questions that you could be asked. They will however, not be the actual questions as they change all the time. Whilst you will be given information about Military entry standards, the Military are particularly coy about releasing too much information regarding aircrew aptitude testing. This is a deliberate act. They want to try to obtain an accurate indication of your innate abilities. Here is a link to a typical brochure available to the general public in relation to aircrew aptitude testing: Military Aptitude Testing Guide[1]

Some completely crumble and others thrive. So we here at Blue Horizon Enterprises will give you a helping hand to complement your innate abilities by giving you the opportunity to become somewhat familiar with the type of questions that will be asked.

Blue Horizon Enterprises have come up with a way that you can prepare easily and affordably in your own home with our **Pilot Aptitude Testing app** which encompasses over 800 questions on the sorts of specific testing that you will face. It allows you to keep score and to record improvements. Whilst we will give you some advice here in this Ebook, this app allows you to interact, which we can't do in a book. It will probably be the best $6 or so you can spend, so check it out here:

ITunes	Google Play

ITunes: https://itunes.apple.com/app/id669233475
G-Play:
https://play.google.com/store/apps/details?id=au.com.getyourwings.aptitudetest.
v2

Our BHE App is dedicated specifically to getting you through pilot Aptitude Testing. If you can master this app you will have a very high probability of getting through this phase of the recruiting. The App covers the typical topics that you will be examined on including:

---

[1] http://content.defencejobs.gov.au/pdf/triservice/DFT_Document_GuideToAptitudeandAbilityTesting_20140402.pdf

✈ **General Ability** General prioritization and mental arithmetic

✈ **Non Verbal Reasoning** Logical thinking

✈ **Mathematics** Ability to think with numbers quickly and accurately

✈ **Specific Aircrew Battery** Cockpit gauge recognition/3D spatial orientation

✈ **Aircrew Co-ordination Exercises** Tilted ball hand-eye coordination

✈ **Typical Psychology Questions** Prepare for the curly questions about yourself

✈ **Typical Interview Questions** Interesting questions that you should be prepared for

The app also neatly simulates time pressure with its in-built countdown clock, which you will meet on the day. More often then not during your testing, the time limit is not quite sufficient, so most people will be forced to rush a little. Sometimes you can even hear the 'tick, tick, tick' as you go. Your confidence will grow as you become accustomed to pilot aptitude type questions under a simulated time pressure. You also will have the ability to score yourself. You will have the ability to practice and improve. You are now at a distinct advantage to those who will see this style of testing for the first time on assessment day. You will only have one chance at this testing, so you need to make it count.

Whilst our App will give you an interactive experience, it is important to state at this point that examples relating to the specific Military pilot aptitude testing in this book are deliberately limited as:

• Test contents do change from time to time,
• This type of testing is difficult to prepare for by design, and

- They are a measure of innate skills rather than rote learnt skills.
- It is impossible to list the exact questions for each nation's Military pilot testing.
- Besides it would not be professional and ethically correct to reveal the exact questions even if we had access to them.

Not all nation's Military aptitude testing is exactly the same but it all follows a very similar model. It is important to remember that the questions we provide are not the exact questions but are very similar to the ones that you will face.

This testing is a crucial element of the recruitment screening, but it is not worth stressing over. Applicants need to ensure that they are relaxed with a clear mind when they commence this testing as it does require the applicant to be able to think logically, quickly and accurately. So get a good sleep the night before. We will now take a closer look at the sorts of topics and questions that you will face on the day by examining each topic individually and giving you examples of the types of questions that you will face. These questions are extracts from our online aircrew aptitude-testing app.

The answers are at the end of the chapter and you will be given a scratch pad for rough notes on the day of testing.

GENERAL ABILITY

These tests are associated with your general reasoning skills and are not aircrew specific but more related to officer aptitude. It basically verifies your education and your level of common sense. Let us give you some examples:

Verbal Reasoning Test Style 1

In this test you will be given 5 questions. You will have 10 minutes available. When you are ready press begin.

Time Allowed   10 minutes

Total   Questions   5

Scoring

- **4 or above**   **Above average**
- **3**   **Average**
- **2 or below**   **Below average**

Typical Questions

1. Julie, Sascha and David have Ferraris.
    David also has a Reliant Robin.
    Jack has a Mercedes and a Model T.
    Will also has a Mercedes.
    Julie also has a Bugatti Veyron.
    Will has just bought a Toyota Prius.

    Who has the fewest cars?
    David   Julie   Sascha   Jack   Will

2. John is double the age of Alfonso and one third as old as Pierre who
    will be 48 years old in 6 years.

    How old is Alfonso?
    7   8   10   11   12

Verbal Reasoning Test Style 2

In this test you will be given 10 questions. You will have 4 minutes available. When you are ready press begin.

Time Allowed   **4 minutes**

Total   Questions   **10**

Scoring

- **7 or above**   **Above average**
- **5-6**   **Average**
- **4 or below**   **Below average**

Typical Questions

1. What is the missing letter in this series:

    a   c   e   ?   i

2. What is the missing letter in this series:

    h   g   ?   e   d

Verbal Reasoning Test Style 3

In this test you will be given 10 questions. You will have 5 minutes available. When you are ready press begin.

Time Allowed   **5 minutes**

Total Questions   **10**

Scoring

- **8 or above**   **Above average**
- **6-7**   **Average**
- **5 or below**   **Below average**

Typical Questions

1. A graduate applying for pilot training with a major airline was asked what he would do if, after a long-haul flight to Sydney, he met the captain wearing a dress in the hotel bar. What would you do?

2. If you have two coins totaling 11c, and one of the coins is not a 1c coin, what are the two coins?
    The following tests are associated with testing your numerical reasoning and logical thinking skills under time pressure.

TYPICAL MATHEMATICS STYLE QUESTIONS

Non-Verbal Reasoning Test 1

In this test you will be given 15 questions. You will have 10 minutes available. When you are ready press begin.

Time Allowed   10 minutes

Total Questions   15

Scoring

- 12 or above   Above average
- 9-10   Average
- 8 or below   Below average

1.   You are traveling at 100 knots. How far will you travel in 45 minutes?

   90 nm   120 nm   150 nm   75 nm   50 nm

2.   You fuel flow is 44 lbs per hour. How much fuel will you burn in 45 minutes?

   44 lb   33 lb   24 lb   12 lb   56 lb

3.   You have 490 lbs of fuel on board. How much fuel will you have left after flying for 37 minutes at a fuel flow of 200 lbs per hour?

   401 lb   367 lb   375 lb   351 lb   309 lb

4.   You are 120 nm from your destination and traveling at 100 knots ground speed with a 20 knot headwind. If you have 129 lbs of fuel on board and a present fuel flow of 45 lb per hour. How much fuel will you have left at your destination?

   73 lb   55 lb   61 lb   66 lb   70 lb

5.   An aircraft flies 930 miles in 75 minutes. How many miles does it fly in 4 hours 45 minutes assuming a constant ground speed?

| 3453 nm | 3534 nm | 3635 nm | 3456 nm | 3258 nm |

6.   The rudder of an aircraft broke off. The part that broke off represented 2/5 of its length. A piece 6 feet long was found left intact. What was the length of the part that broke off?

| 2 ft | 4 ft | 6 ft | 8 ft | 10 ft |

Non-Verbal Reasoning Test 2

In this test you will be given a series of questions related to graphical and tabulated information. You will have 1.5 minutes available per question for a random number of questions. After 1.5 minutes the questions will dissolve if no answer is received and you will automatically move onto the next question. When you are ready press begin.

Time Allowed   **1.5 minutes per question.**

Total Questions   **Random**

Scoring

- **75% or above**   **Above average**
- **65-74 %**   **Average**
- **73 % or below**   **Below average**

PASSAGE A

A taxi driver works 46 weeks of the year and gets an average of 70 customers a week which average 4 miles each at 90 cents per mile.

His expenditure is as follows:

Car Service/repairs/Insurance	$1250 per annum
Diesel Fuel Costs	6 c per mile
Mortgage Costs	$250 per week
Food /electricity	$125 per week

Passage A Q 1   What is the total income in dollars of the taxi driver for the whole year?

Passage A Q 2   What is his total expenditure over the year to the nearest dollar?

Passage A Q 3   What is his average excess of income over expenditure per month to the nearest dollar?

PASSAGE B

The world prices of the main agricultural commodities ($US per tonne) for the period 1985-89 are indicated below.

Commodity	1985	1986	1987	1988	1989
Beef	205	150	155	160	165
Wheat	178	136	112	135	140
Butter	124	84	75	90	98
Maize	120	75	68	80	82
Sugar	10	15	27	42	45

Passage B Q 1   Which two commodities showed the same change in price in 1989 compared to 1985?

Beef and Sugar   Maize and Sugar   Beef and wheat

Wheat and maize   Wheat and sugar

Passage B Q 2   Which commodity has seen the biggest drop in price as a percentage per tonne from 1985 compared to 1989?

Beef   Maize   Wheat   Sugar
Butter

Passage B Q 3	Which commodity has seen the biggest drop in price as a percentage per tonne for any one year?

Beef	Maize	Wheat	Sugar
Butter			

The following topics examine your level of English and ability to quickly analyze information. Both of these skills are essential in the cockpit.

Comprehension Test Style 1

In this test you will be given 3 passages and 12 questions. You will have 12 minutes available. When you are ready press begin.

Time Allowed	12 minutes
Total Questions	12

Scoring

- 8 or above   Above average
- 7   Average
- 6 or below   Below average

PASSAGE A

From reading the background information, please indicate whether the following statement is true, false or not possible to say.

When Christianity was first established by law, a corrupt form of Latin had become the common language of all the western parts of Europe. The service of the Church accordingly, and the translation of the Bible which was read in churches, were both in that corrupted Latin which was the common language of the country. After the fall of the Roman Empire, Latin gradually ceased to be the language of any part of Europe. However, although Latin was no longer understood anywhere by the great body of the people, Church services still continued to be performed in that language. Two different languages were thus established in Europe: a language of the priests and a language of the people.

WINGS | How to Become a Military Pilot

Passage A Q 1 Priests spoke a different language from the common
people.

True
False
Can't say

Passage A Q 2 Latin continued to be used in church services because of
the continuing influence of the Roman Empire.
True
False
Can't say

Passage A Q 3 After the fall of the Roman Empire, most people who
had previously spoken Latin stopped using it.
True
False
Can't say

Passage A Q 4 Prior to the fall of the Roman Empire, Latin had been
established by law as the language of the Church in
western Europe.
True
False
Can't say

PASSAGE B

From reading the background information, please indicate whether the
following statement is true, false or not possible to say.

*At any given moment we are being bombarded by physical and psychological stimuli competing
for our attention. Although our eyes are capable of handling more than 5 million bits of data
per second, our brains are capable of interpreting only about 500 bits per second. With
similar disparities between each of the other senses and the brain, it is easy to see that we must
select the visual, auditory or tactile stimuli that we wish to compute at any specific time.*

Passage B Q 1 Physical stimuli usually win in the competition for our attention.
True
False
Can't say

Passage B Q 2 The capacity of the human brain is sufficient to interpret nearly all the stimuli the sense can register under optimum conditions.
True
False
Can't say

Passage B Q 3 than ears. Eyes are able to cope with greater input of information

True
False
Can't say

Passage B Q 4 time. The brain can compute several stimulate at the same

True
False
Can't say

Comprehension Test Style 2

In this test you will be given 10 questions. You will have 4 minutes available. When you are ready press begin.

Time Allowed   **4 minutes**

Total Questions   10

Scoring

- 8 or above   **Above average**
- 7   **Average**
- 6 or below   **Below average**

Question 1

What order should the following sentences be in so that they run in sequence?

1. *Two cars and a truck had been involved and the highway was blocked.*

2. *Regardless of this, however it was necessary for the crew to get the truck driver out of his cab before they could start clearing the vehicles.*

3. *The fire brigade arrived at the scene of the accident.*

4. *The traffic jam already stretched over 3 kms.*

     a.   3142

     b.   3124

     c.   1342

     d.   3142

Question 2

What order should the following sentences be in so that they run in sequence?

1. *Add the rolled up pullovers, sweaters, T-shirts and lingerie until you have an even surface.*
2. *Then bottom jackets, coats and dresses and place them on top of the trousers.*
3. *Place trousers or skirts at the bottom of the case.*
4. *Carefully fold any overhanging clothing into the case before securing the fasteners.*

     a.   1423

     b.   1432

     c.   3214

     d.   3241

Vocabulary Test 1

In this test you will be given 10 questions. You will have 4 minutes available. When you are ready press begin.

Time Allowed   **4 minutes**

Total Questions   **10**

Scoring

- **8 or above**   **Above average**
- **7**   **Average**
- **6 or below**   **Below average**

1. Replace the question marks with the correct words:

    The victim was ? some ?

a)	offerred	therapy
b)	offered	therapy
c)	oferred	theripy
d)	oferred	therapy
e)	None of these	

2. Replace the question marks with the correct words:

    Everyone was ? ? the witness.

a)	their	except
b)	there	except
c)	they're	except
d)	there	accept
e)	None of these	

Vocabulary Test 2

In this test you will be given 24 questions. You will have 5 minutes available. When you are ready press begin.

Time Allowed   **5 minutes**

Total Questions   **24**

Scoring

- 19 or above   **Above average**
- 17-19   **Average**
- 16 or below   **Below average**

1. Find the best synonym or antonym?
    Infringe
    Discuss   transpire   violate
2. Find the best synonym or antonym?
    Tidy
    Unkempt   engulf   popular
3. Find the best synonym or antonym?
    Conscious
    Irrational   insensible   unmoved
4. Find the best synonym or antonym?
    Obscure
    Relaxed   transparent   comparable

Advanced Vocabulary Test – ENTER WITH CAUTION!

In this test you will be given 22 questions. You will have 5 minutes available. When you are ready press begin.

Time Allowed   **5 minutes**

Total Questions   **22**

Scoring

- **15 or above**   **Above average**
- **11-14**   **Average**
- **10 or below**   **Below average**

Find the words which best describes the following word:

1. *Assuage*

   Argue   decorate   sooth

2. *Pragmatic*

   Practical   argumentative   difficult

3. *Reticent*

   Backward   restrained   awkward

4. *Salubrious*

   Organic solvent   wholesome   salty

Mathematics

These tests determine your numerical logical thinking ability given a time constraint.

Arithmetic Questions

In this test you will be given 10 questions. You will have 12 minutes available. When you are ready press begin.

Time Allowed   **12 minutes**

Total Questions   10

Scoring

- 8 or above   Above average
- 7   Average
- 6 or below   Below average

1.   The ratio of number of boys and girls in a school of 432 students is 5:4. How many new girls should join the school so that the ratio 1:1?

    16   48   60   240

2.   2 men or 3 women can do a piece of work in 10 days. In how many days can 4 men and 3 women do the work together?

    3 ⅓   2 ⅔   3   2 ⅓

3.   If 5 oranges cost 75c, how many can you buy for $2.70?

    15   16   17   18   19

Number Series Test 1

In this test you will be given 10 questions. You will have 10 minutes available. When you are ready press begin.

Time Allowed   10 minutes

Total Questions   10

Scoring

- 8 or above   Above average
- 7   Average
- 6 or below   Below average

1. Complete the sequence by replacing xx with the correct number:

4216　67　2531　74　6252　75　6132　xx

75

76

77

78

79

80

2. Complete the sequence by replacing xx with the correct number:

7　13　25　49　xx

95

96

97

98

99

100

3. Complete the sequence by replacing xx with the correct number:

6　6　8　12　12　24　20　xx　36

15

16

17

18

19

20

4.   Complete the sequence by replacing xx with the correct number:

| 22 | 12 | 10 | 35 | xx | 16 | 34 | 23 | 11 |

36

37

20

19

PSYCHOLOGICAL TESTING

The next series of questions relate to your psychological profile. In this test you will be presented with a range of fairly typical psychology type questions that you will receive on the day. The questions generally come in two formats, but they are basically asking the same thing. They want to know more about you. There is no "correct" answer. The Psychologist is looking for two things. Firstly, they will gain an indication of your personality from your answers and secondly they want consistency. So do you fit the aircrew mould personality wise? Are you truthful by being consistent with your answers and not writing down what you think they want to hear?

The first set of questions may require you to tick on a sliding scale from Strongly Disagree through Agree to Strongly Agree for each question. In the interests of simplicity here, we will simply display some typical questions. We do not intend to analyze your answers so there will be no answers available or recording of score and usually there is no time limit.

The second set again analyzes you by asking you some yes and no questions on a sliding scale. It is important as you may well be asked the same question in your psychology interview which you will have at some stage later. If you are faced with this same question in the interview, it is important that you answers are consistent and can be justified with say an example. They may disguise it by asking it in a different way or as a false negative, ie Instead of What do you like

….. versus what don't you like …. The key here is consistency and honesty. So do the test a few times a few days apart and record your answers elsewhere to see if the answers are the same a few days later. The psychologist is obviously looking for undesirable characteristics, but if you are consistent and honest this is a very positive step. Good luck!

Psychology Test 1 - Agree or Disagree Questions

In this test you will be given 20 questions. When you are ready press begin.

Total Questions   **20**

No Scoring.

Select a response for each question which best describes you:

1   Strongly disagree

2   Disagree

3   Neutral

4   Agree

5   Strongly agree

Questions

1.   I am a creative, ideas person.
2.   I consciously seek, and frequently obtain, leadership roles.
3.   I am normally sympathetic to others and eager to help.
4.   I am sociable, preferring large groups to one to one.
5.   People view me as responsible.
6.   I am very adaptable and resourceful.
7.   I like to focus on the bigger picture rather than fine detail.
8.   I try to avoid taking risks.
9.   I take a positive attitude towards frustration and failure.
10. I am willing to compromise my own view to obtain a group consensus.
11. I like the arts instead of science.
12. I would rather go to the opera than a museum.
13. I would prefer to fly a fighter jet than operate in a crew.

Psychology Test 2 - Yes or No Questions

In this test you will be given 20 questions. When you are ready press begin.

Total Questions   20

No Scoring.

Circle the number that best represents your answer.

1.   **Positively Yes**
2.   **Mostly Yes**
3.   **Undecided**
4.   **Mostly No**
5.   **Positively No**

1.   Is it easy for you to like nearly everyone?

2.   Do you realize your weaknesses and attempt to correct them?

3.   Can you take being teased?

4.   Do you avoid feeling sorry for yourself?

5.   Are you courteous to your fellow workers?

6.   Do you respect the opinions of older family members?

7.   Do you introduce yourself to people easily and correctly?

8.   Do you refrain from pouting when things go differently than you would like?

9.   Do you like children?

10.   Can you work with members that are gay?

11.   How would you deal with a member of your crew who has strong religious beliefs that were not aligned to yours?

I can remember being interviewed by the Psychologist after completing one of these tick and flick questionnaires with similar questions to that above. I remember there were more questions than time so I had to rush a little and I didn't get much time per question, so really

I had to answer with the first thing that came into my head. Anyhow, I didn't realize it but I had somehow managed to fill in the questions leaning towards a tendency to prefer operating on my own. So she asked the question to me directly along the lines of "So would you enjoy flying a fighter jet solo?", I said yes, I would. She then said, 'Well how can you prove to us that you would be comfortable operating in a crew environment as you have clearly stated here that you prefer operating independently?' I stated that it was a marginal preference if anything and I would be very happy with any flying job. I remember talking about athletics and whilst most of my performances were individual and performed to a high level, I enjoyed very much the relays and team events. She seemed happy with that. Funny thing is that she asked my mate the exact opposite question in the interview that he preferred operating in a crew and how would he go independently alone in a fighter – Could he trust himself to do the job? So I guess no matter what you answer, they ask you the opposite.

AIRCRAFT 3-D VISUALIZATION

The next series of tests examine your ability to visualize aircraft in 3 dimensional space, which is an analysis of your innate ability to visualize aircraft in 3 dimensional space. This will ascertain your level of 3D spatial orientation. You will be time compressed so you will have to think relatively quickly. You are the pilot of the aircraft and the aircraft can bank (roll) left or right using aileron, pitch up or down using elevator or yaw left or right about the vertical axis using the rudder. You will need to understand the difference between the various angles of bank 30, 45, 60 and 90 degrees. Don't worry, you will be introduced to the concept right now. You will be provided with 2 cockpit instruments – an attitude indicator (which shows your attitude with reference to the horizon) and a compass that indicates your magnetic heading. Your job is to interpret these instruments and then select 1 of 4 possible aircraft pictorial representations that relates to the readings on the instruments - but you don't get a lot of time.

Compass explanation

North is considered to be flying "into" the page. So an indication of South on the compass would mean the aircraft is depicted as flying out of the page towards you. Likewise East, means the aircraft would be flying towards your right and West is to your left as you look at the page.

Attitude Indicator Explanation

This instrument represents the aircraft in 3D. It is important to look at the aircraft reference the horizon. Firstly is it wings level or pitching up or down? The blue represents sky and the brown represents the ground. By referring to a white triangular sky pointer you can quickly ascertain whether the aircraft has any bank angle (ie turning left or right). Often it is a combination of pitching and rolling. Your aim is to interpret these instruments reasonably quickly.

3D Spatial Orientation Testing

The following images are screenshots of our online app. From your interpretation of the Compass and Attitude Indicator below, select the best orientation of the aircraft from the choices available that match the instruments. There is only one correct answer.

You will have 6 minutes to complete 18 questions (20 seconds per question). When you are ready press begin.

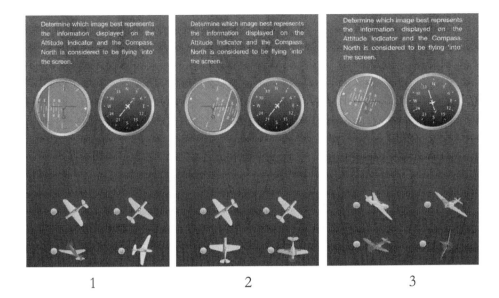

1   2   3

COCKPIT INSTRUMENT INTERPRETATION

This test checks your ability to read 3 typical cockpit aircraft instruments: RPM (Revolutions Per Minute), Oil Pressure and Oil Temperature. These are generic instruments and your test could utilize any instruments in the cockpit. You will be given a relatively short time of 5 seconds to examine the instruments and provide the answer to a fairly specific parameter before the instruments disappear from the screen. This represents a situation where you have an aircraft problem and only a limited time to solve it. The key is to look at only the instrument asked and how the scale of units works for that particular instrument. It does not require an advanced understanding of aircraft instruments. However, read the question and study the scale. Rushing is not good here. Double check your answers. Remember the real test has the screen go blank after 3-5 seconds, so try to only look at the image for that time period to simulate the test.

There is only one correct answer. You will have 3 minutes to complete 25 questions. When you are ready press begin.

Time remaining

Question number

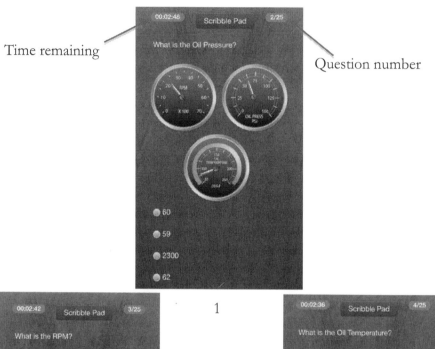

1

2

3

AIRCREW COORDINATION EXERCISE

This exercise is a fairly typical aircrew specific coordination exercise. You will have partial control of a red ball. For actual testing this is usually achieved by you being seated in a chair at a console. You will have a stick between your legs, which moves the ball up and down and a set of rudder pedals which move it left or right. You may also have a joystick, which seems 'oversensitive' and you will only have partial control of the ball.

For the simulation contained within our app, you can control the ball via tilting your phone or tablet. The aim is to keep the ball in the centre grey shaded circle for as long as possible. You will get the hang of it quickly. You will have 2 x 30 sec periods. The blue box represents the time left and the black box represents for how many seconds the ball has been in the middle. The aim is to gain improvement from the first period to the second. The normal gain is in the vicinity of 25%. You should aim for higher. Our app has 3 levels. Hard level is for experts only. Good Luck!

Below are screenshots only to give you an indication of what your test could look like.

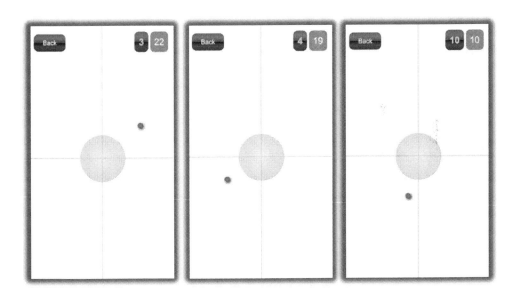

ESSAY

A fairly typical task given to new Military pilot aspirants is to demonstrate your written communication skills in English. You will be asked to write an essay within approximately a 30 minutes time period. There will be a plethora of topics that you can choose to write the essay about. Topics used previously include:

- ✈ **Leadership.** Are leaders born or made? What makes a good leader? What leadership characteristics do you have and provide some examples?

- ✈ **World War II.** What do you know about WWII? What role did your country have in the outcome and who were the main leaders of your country at that time?

- ✈ **Communication.** What makes an effective communicator? Are you one? Describe a situation where teamwork and good communication skills solved the issue. Describe your communication style and in what areas you can improve.

- ✈ **Expectations.** What expectations do you have in becoming a pilot in the Military? How did you come to your decision and what drive and dedication do you have to achieve that goal?

- ✈ **Military memorial day.** What do you know about the day that your nation stops to remember it's fallen? Have you taken part in one of these days before, if so what was your role? What were your recollections and what does this day mean for you?

- ✈ **Motivation.** Why you want to join the Military? What strengths, weaknesses and personal qualities do you bring and what evidence do you have so far in your life that demonstrates your suitability to become a Military pilot.

However, these topics do change from time to time but are along the same theme. They are looking here for an indication of your level of written communication. Are you neat or do you leave chicken scratchings all over the paper. Do you use slang, do you have good grammar, expression and vocabulary. This essay shows a lot about you, so practice a few and get them looked at by a critical third party. Try to write neatly. Don't try to use big words, just be yourself. Often writing about a personal experience makes it easier.

It is also important to remember that no matter what language you speak, you will do your pilot's course in English as this is the international aviation language and all pilots need to be fluent in English. Most technical manuals and Air Traffic Clearances will be written in English.

TYPICAL INTERVIEW QUESTIONS

You will do all or a random mix of the testing as detailed in the chapter so far. At some stage on the process you will be required to have a formal interview with Military personnel, which is normally as a minimum, a trained Military Interviewing Officer (IO). They want to know more about you in addition to your testing results and what you have written down so far in your application paperwork. This may be an interview with just you and the IO or could be more formal such as a formal interview board. This interview will be required for entry and the board could consist of an IO, a senior Military officer (normally aircrew) and a Psychologist. The comments written after this interview are valued as they assess the applicant's Military suitability and officer qualities. Among other topics, IO's need to provide direct feedback on you to the approving authority. Some mebers of BHE were IO. We will now list typical contents of an IO's checklist, so that you can be ready to answer these questions.

IO Checklist

Motivation to join the Military. All trainees face difficulty at some time. What is the strength of their motivation, as it can mean the difference between a pass and a fail? What is their real motivation to fly...not just "I have always wanted to be a pilot". What have they done to demonstrate a long held interest in aviation? (model aircraft, courses of study, Military cadets, etc).
What does the applicant find appealing about the Military? Does the applicant have a genuine interest in the Military apart from being a pilot? You should have already prepared for these questions at initial recruiting application day.
Level of knowledge and expectations of Military life. Knowledge is an indirect indicator of motivation and expectations. Are the expectations of the

candidate realistic, and if so, on what basis? How well has it been researched? What effort has the applicant made?

Potential compatibility service life. What evidence is there in the applicant's current lifestyle to indicate they would adjust to service life?

Setbacks. How well do they deal with setbacks? Can they provide any evidence of successful setback resolution?

Personal Qualities. They need to be convinced that you have the ability to get on with others and work effectively in a group and that you have a proven high level of personal organization. They will also want to appraise your ability to prioritize and plan, your resilience to stress, your ability to adapt quickly to new and rapidly changing situations. Most of these criteria can be answered in your

exposure to an educational institution or perhaps in your recent employment if that has been the case. So think about examples of each of these points so that you are ready to go with an example.

The IO or selection board will be required to file a report indicating comments on Military compatibility, knowledge of service applied for, interest and understanding of the job, and the training you are about to undertake, adjustment and assimilation potential and overall presentation.

Any member of the panel can ask any question. At the end of the interview, the Defence Interviewer will score your performance. A typical score could be from 1 to 7 with 1 being unacceptable (and do not reapply), 4 acceptable and 7 being outstanding, but you will not be shown this rating. Remember they are trying to recruit an officer first, pilot second.

If you are being interviewed to go to a Military Academy then they may well ask some questions in additional areas. Here are a typical list of boxes contained on a IO's checklist sheet that will need to be commented upon by the IO or board. Again, have a think about the answers that you will provide and practice before going for the interview.

- ☑ Is person likely to be committed to a Military life and the profession of arms?

- ☑ Does the candidate really want to be a Military officer and pursue an Military career?

- ☑ Why do they value a Military career?

- ☑ Does the candidate want to lead others?

- ☑ How confidently can we predict that the candidate will cope with Military and academic demands?

- ☑ Does the candidate want a University degree?

- ☑ Confirmation and validation of an individual's history?

- ☑ Do the records indicate a disciplined approach to study?

- ☑ Do they have the energy to cope with the long hours of work?

- ☑ Are they well organized to plan his/her approach to work?

- ☑ Are they coping with studies and enjoying sport and social activities at the same time already?

- ☑ Can they cope with personal and interpersonal demands of living with many others?

- ☑ Can they meet the high standard of housekeeping?

- ☑ Do they value physical fitness?

- ☑ Are the actively engaged in sport or physical activity?

- ☑ Can they relate to the peer group?

☑ Are they gregarious, free from abrasive words or mannerisms likely to provoke others, will they prove cooperative?

☑ Is the candidate a female? Does she have the confidence in her ability to cope as an equal when she will be outnumbered? Can she mix easily with males?

They may also discuss any of the following topics with you to ensure awareness and to check your level of understanding and acceptance.

Typical items discussed include:

✈ Combat Role and what it means to you.

✈ Nature of primary duties.

✈ Commitment to fixed period of service (ROSO).

✈ NMUD Policy (Non Medical Use of Drugs such as marijuana, narcotics, etc).

✈ Defence Force alcohol policy.

✈ Fitness policy.

✈ Defence Force Discipline Act (DFDA).

✈ Equal Opportunity Employment environment (EEO).

✈ What is unacceptable behaviour?

✈ Criminal history.

✈ Pay and what they expect to be paid.

✈ Military Superannuation and Pension Scheme.

✈ Relationships (same sex/de-facto).

✈ Partner's employment.

✈ Postings (notification of relocation to a new role and/or location).

✈ Discharge and removals policy.

✈ Accommodation.

- ✈ Outstanding medical issues.

- ✈ Length of training.

- ✈ GSK (General Service Knowledge).

- ✈ Financial situation.

- ✈ Ongoing family issues.

Remember, most of this you will have already covered before going into recruiting and you should have already thought about these topics before this interview rather than face them for the first time today! In addition, a large amount of this information is contained in this book and it can also be found on the website links associated with your Military. So put in some effort and take a few notes and at least have a think about answers to some of the issues raised here so that you will be ready for those sorts of questions. You don't need to know everything of course, but some knowledge will go a long way. They will not expect a detailed understanding of all policies such as Defence Force Discipline Act, Defence Force policy on alcohol and non-medical use of drugs, but they want to know that you are aware of them and are willing to accept them.

The interview is important but don't sweat it too much. Do your homework and be honest. They want to see a smart looking, confident candidate, who has done some research and has a strong desire to be a pilot. No doubt you will get a question that you don't know the answer to. If so, be truthful and say that you don't know, rather than try to guess or lie your way out of it. The content of your answers should be honest and from the heart. Don't tell them what you think they want to hear. Remember to smile and look them in the eye. Your body language here can say a lot about you. Don't slouch, fold your arms and look away when being spoken to. Sit upright, look confident yet relaxed and try to enjoy the interview. You would not be in this room if they didn't think that you had a chance.

Don't forget, like the psychologist, the Interviewing Officer will have all the information regarding your testing results so far at their fingertips, including your answers to the psychologist's questions – so be consistent! They may ask you how you feel you went, so be honest as they already know themselves. You will also get a chance to ask questions regarding the Military. These questions should be basic and non-controversial. Intelligent questions of your own shows that you have given thought to what your life will be like in the Military and that you haven't just 'crammed' for an interview and thought about it yesterday. Never allow yourself to become flustered, tense or defensive, just relax, smile, just tell the truth and be yourself. Don't pretend to be someone you are not. It is much harder!

SAMPLE INTERVIEW QUESTIONS

Here is a sample list of the sort of questions that you can expect to face during the recruiting process. It may not be the actual questions you will be asked, just combined examples from personal experiences and previous applicants. This is a typical list and generic in nature. No doubt you will get many other questions not listed here, but this is an indication of the style of questions that you will face. Don't forget that they are looking not only at the content of your answers, but your mannerisms and delivery. They need to be convinced of your long held desire to be an officer in the Military first and a pilot second. What evidence can you give them that this is the case? The board will look at your achievements so far to determine a prediction of how you will cope with the demands of the Military and the challenge of pilot's course.

Hot Tip

Video tape yourself being asked some of these questions by your parents or a colleague. Try to make it realistic by sitting in a chair and when you receive the question, try to make eye contact with your screen and deliver a reasonably quick but thoughtful reply. Your answer should make sense, be honest and logical. Don't try to be someone else. If you are video recording, then you should also look for poor eye contact, shuffling or fidgeting, poor posture and silly facial expressions. So when you are ready sit back relax and just be yourself. Remember, there are no correct answers, everyone is different!

PERSONAL

- ✈ Why do you want to become a Military pilot?

- ✈ Have you discussed your decision to join the Military with your family? How do they feel?

- ✈ What would your parents say about you?

- ✈ What do your parents expect of you?

- ✈ How did your mother and father influence your life?

- ✈ Describe your family and childhood?

- ✈ What kind of person are you?

- ✈ Are you well organized? Provide examples.

- ✈ Are you co-operative or abrasive? Provide examples.

- ✈ How do you relate to groups and how do you work with members of the opposite sex? Provide examples.

- ✈ What are your hobbies? What do you do in your spare time?

- ✈ Where do you see yourself in 15 years?

- ✈ Do you know anybody in the Military? If so, what would they say about you?

- ✈ Do you have high levels of self discipline and a high energy level? Provide examples.

- ✈ Who do you admire most (someone you would use as a role model)? What do you admire most about them?

- ✈ What would your partner/spouse say is your greatest fault?

- ✈ What is the biggest mistake you have ever made?

- ✈ What sports are you involved in?

- ✈ Do you value physical fitness?

- ✈ Describe your current level of fitness?

- ✈ How will you cope with the loss of personal privacy?

GENERAL MILITARY QUESTIONS

- ✈ Do you have a preferred service, if so, which one and why?

- ✈ How would you feel if you were offered entry into a service within an arm of the Military which is not your first choice?

- ✈ What do you have to offer the Military?

- ✈ How would you feel if we offered you a position in Air Traffic Control or an Engineer?

- ✈ Why do you want to join the Military?

- ✈ What can you tell us about the Military?

- ✈ What do you find appealing about becoming an officer?

- ✈ If you are not successful at pilot training, what will you do?

- ✈ Why not become a civilian pilot? Don't they pay better!

- ✈ What do you know about the training you are about to undertake?

- ✈ Why should we hire you over all the other candidates?

- ✈ How did you prepare for this interview?

- ✈ If you had a choice, what aircraft would you like to fly? Why?

- ✈ What do you think makes the difference between an average officer and a very good officer?

- ✈ What makes a good leader?

- ✈ What is the difference between leadership and management?

- ✈ Can leadership be taught?

- ✈ What are the different styles of leadership? What style are you?

- ✈ Give an example of a good leader. Why?

- ✈ If you are not successful, what do you think would be the most likely reason?

- ✈ Where are our fighter aircraft mainly based and what aircraft fly there?

→ How many frontline fighter aircraft do we have?

→ What aircraft does our Formation Aerobatic team fly?

→ How would you handle being away from home most of the time?

→ Would you be prepared to go to war?

→ How do flaps work on an aircraft?

→ What role do Chinook helicopters have in the Army?

→ What's the difference between a piston and turbo prop aircraft?

→ What is your understanding of the Defence Force Discipline Act?

→ How will you cope with Military discipline?

→ What is your expectation of your lifestyle associated with joining the Military?

→ What is the rank structure of the Military?

→ Who is the current Defence Minister?

→ What is the Military policy on drugs?

→ What is the main rifle used by members of the Military?

→ What is meant by 'Combat Role'?

→ How much will you be paid during your training?

→ How much leave will you get per year?

→ What position are you interested in after obtaining your wings?

→ What will your daily routine be like in that role?

→ How do you feel about changing locations every 2-3 years?

OFFICER TRAINING

→ What and where is our Military academy?

→ If you had a choice, what degree would you undertake and why?

→ What is Common Military training?

✈ What is Single service training?

✈ Explain a typical day at our Military academy?

✈ What personal restrictions will be placed on you during your training?

✈ Where are the respective Single Service officer Training facilities?

✈ What is the duration of these courses?

✈ Describe what you expect to learn from this course?

✈ How will you handle the late nights, early starts and endless inspections?

✈ Can you mix study and other activities? Provide examples.

✈ What are your study habits like now?

✈ Can you resign and if so when?

✈ How will you cope with less sleep?

CURRENT AFFAIRS

You can also expect some questions regarding Military related current affairs. In particular things like impending aircraft acquisitions, latest operational activities and any other items which would make the newspapers in relation to Military activities in your country. This is where work experience would be invaluable as you would be in a position to ask questions here (within reason) to try to learn as much as you can about what the Military is all about and what your role in it would be.

WHAT'S NEXT?

The next stage in the recruiting process is variable depending upon your nation and which arm of the Military you intend to join. However what can be said is that after the pilot specific aptitude Testing day, you will be notified via letter of your results of this testing usually within 2 weeks. For some Military organizations, that letter will detail a date for your Officer Selection Board (OSB) which can be the last phase of testing before being appointed into the Military for officer training. Some militaries require further testing before formal induction. Some Militaries require applicants who have been successful and performed well at pilot aptitude assessment day to compete for a position on a Flight Screening Program (FSP) to ascertain airborne learning potential.

If you get a 'no' letter after your pilot aptitude testing, don't despair. Perhaps it says 'not at this time', we should know, one of us got two! If you are keen, apply again in 12 months time. It almost is another test they are giving you. Many Military pilots have done this. Indeed it is looked upon quite favourably if you do reapply, especially if you have achieved something tangible in between like attended and successfully completed a course or been involved in gainful employment. You will be asked the question, "So what have you been doing in the last 12 months". Be ready to answer it with something positive.

I am afraid we can't help you if you get a DCM letter (Don't Come Monday), thanks, but no thanks letter. Sometimes this happens, it could be that there was a significant issue in your testing such as an undiagnosed medical problem or other issue. You will rarely if ever be given any feedback on the specific reason, but if your letter says, thank you, but no and no reapplications will be processed from you, then hey you have no doubt given it your best and despite our advice and assistance and your hard work, Military aviation is just not for you. Bummer. There is always civilian aviation or perhaps another job in the Military.

THE FLIGHT SCREENING PROGRAM (FSB) AND THE OFFICER SELECTION BOARD (OSB)

We are well on the way now. For some nations, you will go direct to a pre-convened OSB, the final stage of the recruitment process. Other nations require you to complete an FSP, which encompasses both the assessed flying element and the OSB. We will cover both scenarios.

Now it is time to do some flying! This is where you will tackle the final components associated with a typical Military pilot selection process. It is normally the last stage of the vetting process and being successful here means that you get to have a crack at pilot's course after your officer training and it is your key that could open the door to a fantastic Military career.

All applicants attending an FSP or OSB will be ranked based on results from the recruitment process so far. Normally the Military 'skim' the best applicants from the top of the applicant pool. It is these top candidates that normally fill the vacant positions as they come up on the FSP. You are normally held in the pool for say 12 months, or you could be called up quite quickly, so you need to be ready to move. If not selected for a FSP within 12 months, then it would be best to contact your local recruiting centre to determine the status of your application. You may be in the lower percentile of candidates. Those applicants selected for FSP will be allocated to the next available course (try to make your self available!). You will be informed in writing, along with joining instructions which detail where, when, what, items to bring, etc.

Let us just say that you would not be about to undertake some flying that will cost the Military significant money, if they didn't think that you had a very good chance of making it. So you are obviously doing something right! Keep it up, they like what they see so far, but it is not over yet. Remember you will normally only get one attempt at the FSP, so be prepared as best you can. Once again, we will give you our advice about how to do well on this course.

It is important to note that on some occasions, successful completion of the FSP may lead to an immediate appointment into the Military so you need to be 'locked and loaded' and ready to start your officer training very quickly wherever that may be.

THE FLIGHT SCREENING PROGRAM

A Military sanctioned flying unit facilitates the FSP and it has a Military flying program specifically designed for testing Military pilot aptitude. It is normally completed in single engine piston aircraft by professional Military or civilian ex-Military flying instructors who know exactly what they are looking for. The program could be divided into two courses, Basic and Advanced, depending upon your previous flying experience. The delineator is usually around 20 hours of airborne experience.

BHE Gouge (Our Advice)

The authors recommend that all applicants undertake some flying in a light aircraft prior to the FSP, so that you have at least experienced the airborne environment. This means do some flying before you formally apply to recruiting as the whole recruiting process could be quite fast for a strong candidate. It is not necessary to enrol in any training, but just to go for a couple of joys flights at the very least. A basic knowledge of what a circuit consists of (i.e. crosswind, downwind, base and final for instance) would show the Military instructor that you have bothered to at least learn a bit. What is a yoke (control wheel) and what happens to the aircraft when you push the yoke forward, or turn it to the left? What is a rudder, an aileron or a stall? How does the radio work? You will learn an amazing amount just going for a fly. You don't really want your first mission on the FSP to be your first airborne experience especially if you technicolor yawn (throw up or barf). Find this out at Seymour Butts Flying School down the road, not on a formal Military flying assessment.

Ideally 15-18 hours flying, whilst expensive would provide you with some exposure to the airborne environment and yet you would still most probably be in the 'basic' category for the FSP. Also you will most probably not have learnt any bad habits by then. But for goodness sake, don't think that you are Tom Cruise either. You will know less than 0.001% of what your instructor will know and the last person they want is a know-it-all. This amount of flying will depend upon your finances as you can expect to pay over $150 per flying hour in civilian aviation. Remember that you will only get one attempt at the FSP and less than 20 hours means that you will be assessed against people who may have never even seen an aircraft up close before. Having said that, it is not a competition against your mates or girlfriends. If you all make the grade, that's good for you and the Military. They would love a 'gun' (high quality) course where everybody is considered a flying 'whip' (expert) and is hired.

A typical FSP in either the basic or advanced course will encompass about 15 hours of flight time and the course takes about two weeks (weather dependent). You will do approximately 10 basic air trainer sorties (flights) with the 6th and 10th normally being a check ride. You could also be asked to complete two simulator sorties in an IF (Instrument Flying) Synthetic Trainer. Each sortie is roughly one hour and 15 minutes duration. FSP scores are awarded on a per sequence basis for a number of sortie profiles including effects of controls, climbing, descending, turning, stalls, circuits and some basic aerobatics like loops and barrel rolls. The profiles are designed to assess aptitude for the airborne environment with particular emphasis on suitability for subsequent training as a Military pilot. Do you listen well (Whilst the radio is going and the loud engine running)? Can you learn and improve quickly? Are you aware of what is going on around you? Can you retain information easily, that sort of thing. A raw mean score (RMS) is derived at the end of an applicant's FSP. For the Basic course this is an average of scored sequences over about 98 profiles, while for the Advanced course the average is about 115 profiles. Although these scores are indicative of aptitude and suitability for training as a Military pilot, the FSP overall assessment also relies heavily on the qualitative assessment of applicants made by FSP flying and ground instructors. In particular how the applicant has demonstrated:

- a high rate of learning,
- an ability to simultaneously think and fly,
- an ability to respond to instruction,
- personal application,
- attitude,
- motivation, and
- maturity.

On the last day of this two-week flying program, applicants will normally be interviewed by the Officer Selection Board to assess overall suitability for entry into the Military as a pilot.

OFFICER SELECTION BOARD (OSB)

At the Officer Selection Board (OSB), all applicants are put through the final phase of the testing. This may involve any one or a combination of group activities, problem solving exercises, verbal presentation exercises and a formal interview. This is difficult to prepare for but again they just want to get to know you and see how you perform as a public speaker and in a group environment. It is important to just keep it simple and be yourself. They don't expect you to be like Chuck Yeager, so just act normal.

You will be given an opportunity to lead and to follow during group activities. So be positive and confident with your leadership opportunities, but it is also important to be a good listener and clear thinker. Remember, when you are not leading an exercise, give the appropriate support to whoever is leading at the time. The Military is about working together as a team and hierarchy and respect are very important. This will be borne out in the problem solving exercises, which require lateral thinking, initiative and good communication skills. You may then be given an opportunity for public speaking with an audience of both your peers and the Selection officers, where the aim is to speak about yourself, perhaps your school, family or life experiences. They just want to see your posture, confidence and ability to project the English language with minimal preparation. It is generally quite short, normally only a few minutes. This is something that you could practice at home with say your parents listening. Don't rush, ensure that you project your voice confidently and that you look at your audience.

The Officer Selection Board Interview itself is normally the last stage of the process. In some cases, the OSB may be done at the end of the pilot assessment day. If your selection process did not conduct the OSB at assessment day, then now is your chance! Reread our earlier notes in this chapter as we have already provided very detailed advice about what to expect on the OSB. To sum up, the OSB is normally conducted in a welcoming environment and usually lasts around an hour, sometimes a little shorter. **You would not be at this stage if you didn't have the potential to be a pilot.** This is a chance for the board to get to know you. It is also important to remember that it can also be a lot of fun, so go into it with an open mind and a sense of humor. Relax, be natural and be yourself.

Further hot tips

→ *Be confident. The Military is looking for someone who is self-confident and someone who believes they can do the job. Remember though, confident is NOT arrogant.*

→ *Always be honest. Give honest answers and don't be afraid to say you don't know. The Military is not for everyone. If you tell them what you think they want to hear and are not true to yourself, you may still get in but will probably find the Military is not what you are looking for after all.*

✈ *Relax. As well as the content of your answers, interviewers will be looking at you and your body language, so look at them when you answer the question. Sit in a relaxed, open pose and remember to enjoy yourself. Smile but don't overdo it!*

They may well announce the final result of your overall testing at the end of your board. In any result, each applicant will be sent a letter at some stage saying 'Congratulations, you have been selected for pilot and officer training' and for some nations, it will detail into which service that offer relates to. You will be advised details of when and where your training starts. Some may get a letter stating that you meet the required standard and have been placed on a waiting list. For those not selected, it may be 'not selected at this time' in which case plan to apply again and tell them you will, when eligible. You may also get a 'Don't Come back' recommendation. For those applicants unsuccessful at the OSB for Military pilot, you almost made it, try to find out if you passed FSP. If you did then you may be able to re-apply at a later time. If you received a no letter and did not pass the FSP, then despite your positive performance at the pilot assessment day, we are afraid that your aspirations to become a Military pilot have just been snuffed out. Sorry about that.

CONCLUSION

Phew! As you can see the Military recruiting process for aircrew is an exhaustive and extensive process. The Military is about to give you a job for more than a decade and spend millions of taxpayers money on you. So therefore, the Military are prepared to spend significant time and resources to ensure they get the right people. There is no need to become overwhelmed with it all, just stick to the basics. Do your research, know what you are getting yourself into, look smart and be keen and on time. If you don't make it the first time, then try again. The Military recruiting centre may give you some indication of your shortcomings if any, so work on it and have another go. Many of today's badged pilots had two or three attempts until successful at the recruiting process.

Whilst the recruiting process does sound daunting, the Military will always want pilots, particularly the Air Force. After all, somebody has to do the job and you may be just the person they are looking for. They have some fantastic hardware to fly, so get to it! You now have the information laid out before you and you have made a good start by obtaining this book! Remember: Knowledge Empowers You. It is the 'KEY'. Good luck!

I was obviously very disappointed but I wasn't all that surprised when I received the first letter telling me I was not competitive at the present time. I didn't feel confident about it when I was going through the recruiting process and I think it just came down to my level of maturity. I tried again the next year and felt better about it all but I still got a knock-back. After that I was determined to give it another go. By my third attempt, I was all over the subject matter and had the maturity to show them that I was worth the training risk. Receiving that 'Yes' letter was an awesome feeling. It turned out that my perseverance paid off and I ended up having a great flying career in the Air Force. I certainly would have regretted it had I given up after my first attempt.

FURTHER USEFUL INFORMATION

Here are some generic book titles that may be of assistance:

- ✈ *'Military Flight Aptitude Tests' by CliffsTestPrep*[2]
- ✈ *'Check your own IQ' by HJ Eysenck*[3]
- ✈ *'Masterful Mindbenders' by Trevor Thuran*[4]
- ✈ *'ARCO Military Flight Aptitude Tests' by Colonel Solomon Wiener*[5]

Here are some useful IQ/Military aptitude type test websites to get you started:

- ✈ http://www.adfmentors.com.au
- ✈ http://www.kent.ac.uk/careers/psychotests.htm
- ✈ http://www.analyzemycareer.com/index.php?option=com_content&view=article&id=8&Itemid=437
- ✈ http://www.aptitudeonline.co.uk/test/test.html

And don't forget our interactive pilot aptitude testing app designed just for you available at

- ✈ Google Play
  https://play.google.com/store/apps/details?id=au.com.getyourwings.aptitudetest.v2
- ✈ ITunes
  https://itunes.apple.com/app/id669233475

If you want to try to enter the Military in Australia or New Zealand, then we have written a detailed book about the entire process all the way from a desire to be a pilot to retiring as a pilot. Now there are many books out there out there about how to get into the Military mostly written by recruiters, non-aircrew and even contracted authors on behalf of the Military.

---

[2] http://www.amazon.com/CliffsTestPrep-Military-Flight-Aptitude-Tests/dp/076454103X

[3] https://books.google.com.au/books?id=JVG-QgAACAAJ&dq=check+your+own+iq&hl=en&sa=X&ei=LgAPVaCiClbdPfazgKgD&ved=0CCYQ6AEwAA

[4] http://www.amazon.com/Masterful-Mindbenders-TREVOR-TRURAN/dp/0862731267

[5] http://www.waterstonesmarketplace.com/Military-Flight-Aptitude-Tests-Colonel-Solomon-Wiener/book/25451135

Except one book, our book:
WINGS – How to become a Pilot in the ADF

This book was written by us, the team at Blue Horizon Enterprises, your QFI mentors. This book goes into great detail about how to prepare yourself before you go into Military recruiting the first time as well as recruiting tips and what to expect in your life as a pilot both in the Military and after it. It is based on the Australian Defence Force experience. Here is a brief Chapter synopsis:

Chapter 1   ADF Entry Requirements
Chapter 2   ADF Pilot Entry Options
Chapter 3   The Recruiting Process
Chapter 4   Australian Defence Force Academy
Chapter 5   ADF Direct Entry Officer Training
Chapter 6   Basic Flying Training School
Chapter 7   No 2 Flying Training School
Chapter 8   Tips to Passing Pilot's Course
Chapter 9   A Pilot's Life
Chapter 10   Service Facts
Chapter 11 $$$ and benefits of the ADF
Chapter 12   Post ADF – Your Options
Chapter 13   Frequently Asked Questions

You can even download a couple of chapters for free at:
http://www.getyourwings.com.au/about.php

Much of the content of this Australian EBook is based primarily on the personal experiences of the Blue Horizon Enterprises Team as students, officers, Military QFI and Flying/officer Supervisory staff at various training units throughout the Military. We offer you, the budding Military pilot, the benefit of the many years of techniques, tips, anecdotes, mistakes and trial and error gleaned from thousands of flights here in the one place. We have done our best to condense our body of accumulated experience and hope that it goes some way towards mentally and physically preparing you for Military pilot's course.

Answers to Aptitude Questions

GENERAL ABILITY

Verbal Reasoning Test Style 1
1. Answer   **Sascha, Ferrari only.**

2. Answer   **Alfonso is 7 years old.**

Verbal Reasoning Test Style 2
1. Answer   **c**
2. Answer   **f**

Verbal Reasoning Test Style 3
1. Answer   **The captain was a woman.**
2. Answer   **10 c and 1c, the other coin is a 1c.**

Non-Verbal Reasoning Test 1
1. Answer   **75 nm**
2. Answer   **33 lb**
3. Answer   **367 lb**
4. Answer   **61 lb**
5. Answer   **3534 nm**
6. Answer   **4 ft**

Non-Verbal Reasoning Test 2
1. Passage A Q 1 Answer   **$11592**
2. Passage A Q 2 Answer   **$11523**
3. Passage A Q 2 Answer   **$6 per month**
4. Passage B Q 1 Answer   **Wheat and maize**
5. Passage B Q 2 Answer   **Maize**
6. Passage B Q 3 Answer   **Maize**

Comprehension Test Style 1

1. Passage A Q 1 Answer **True**
2. Passage A Q 2 Answer **False**
3. Passage A Q 3 Answer **True**
4. Passage A Q 4 Answer **False**
5. Passage B Q 1 Answer **Can't say**
6. Passage B Q 2 Answer **False**
7. Passage B Q 3 Answer **Can't say**
8. Passage B Q 4 Answer **False**

Comprehension Test Style 2

1. Answer **3142**
2. Answer **3214**

Vocabulary Test Style 1

1. Answer **offered** therapy
2. Answer **there** except

Vocabulary Test Style 2

1. Answer **violate**
2. Answer **unkempt**
3. Answer **insensible**
4. Answer **transparent**

Advanced Vocabulary Test

1. Answer **sooth**
2. Answer **practical**
3. Answer **restrained**
4. Answer **wholesome**

Mathematics Arithmetic Test

1. Answer **48**

2. Answer   **3 ⅓**

3. Answer   **18 oranges**

Number Series Test 1

1. Answer   **76**
2. Answer   **97**
3. Answer   **20**
4. Answer   **19**

3 D Spatial Orientation

1. Answer   **Top right. 90 bank, nose high, heading towards top right (030 deg)**
2. Answer   **Top right. 75 bank, nose high, heading towards top right (030 deg)**
3. Answer   **Bottom right. 45 bank, slight nose low, heading out of page (170 deg)**

CHAPTER 3
Preparation Before Pilot's Course

I knew that I wanted to be a pilot since pre – school age. To learn to fly you could either go the civilian way (pay your own way) or take up the more competitive Defence Force option. In year 10, I rang recruiting (no internet in those days!) to ensure that I was doing the right subjects just in case I wanted to apply. I kept my head down in years 11 and 12. I read that the Air Force were about to buy the FA/18 Hornet fighter jet and I managed to see one perform locally. I thought, "How cool is that". So I applied never really thinking that I would have a chance, but I wanted it and I was prepared to work hard to get it. I went into recruiting not really knowing what to expect but gave all the testing my best shot. I was thrilled when I got a letter late in year 12 to say I had a job as an Air Force cadet and a chance to become a Military pilot. All I had to do was attend the Academy first and get paid to earn a degree.

You need to be prepared to work hard over a long period and you need to be prepared for change. One of the major areas that you will have to change is your method of study. You need to be able to commit much of the information on pilot's course to your long term memory (or hard drive), so that tasks become almost automatic. Think of playing the piano. Once you can do it – it becomes rapid, automatic and allows extra brainspace to do other things at the same time, like conducting a meaningful conversation. If you need to use conscious, direct thought, our brain is limited, potentially slow and can be considered to be a single channel processor (RAM or short term memory) in a multi-channel world.

The Military use an old school saying which is relevant here. It is called the six P's.

'Prior Preparation Prevents Piss Poor Performance.'

The only way to place information into this long-term memory is by repetition, determination and hard work. There are a few things you can examine regarding your own preparation technique before commencing pilot's course. A good time to look at this is prior to recruiting, if it's not too late, as these skills will help you there as well. Let's discuss some of them now.

➤ **Think about the way you study now.** Are you are a 'cram and dump' kind of person? In other words, do you fill your short-term memory with knowledge then delete it ready for the next upload? That technique will not work on pilot's course. A more appropriate way of studying on pilot's course is to understand a subject, so that you will never forget it. We call this 'experiential' learning as if we can understand it, practice it and even do it or experience it, then you are far more likely to remember it. Much of the required learning will require instant mental recollection in conjunction with appropriate and co-ordinated hands and feet movement. Thus you will be 'experiencing' it. Some things are learned by long hours of repetition. A good example is checklists which must be flawlessly committed to long-term memory. If you do not have organized study patterns, you will need to develop them. Specific study techniques to help you are discussed later in this EBook.

➤ **Sharpen your mental arithmetic.** If you are not very good at number crunching simple mathematics quickly with ongoing distractions, then you should start to practice now. Examples of ways to do this might be rolling 2 dice, multiplying their numbers together quickly whilst spinning a pen in your other hand, or adding distances of 3 towns on the same road sign together whilst driving past and listening to the stereo, or, if your speedo says 100 km/h and you see 55 km to go, how many minutes will it take to get there? Try doing your tables whilst on the treadmill. Practicing speed and accuracy with basic number crunching will help.

✈ **Minimize distractions.** Sort out any issues of a domestic nature (eg. car mechanical problems, accommodation issues, trouble with partner, financial issues, etc) before commencing course. It will free up your headspace and ensure that the domestic things get done rather than get ignored and potentially build up to adversely impact on your time and mental state. It is certainly beneficial to have at least a year of smooth sailing domestically in order to cope with the workload.

✈ **Prepare your partner if you have one.** You will need to be working at home most nights for at least 3 hours and spending some hours on the weekends with your head in the books. Your partner needs to understand that this critical element of your training requires plenty of study time, minimal distractions and absolute concentration. You may even be able to involve your partner, (if you have one) to help you. For example, they can read out a limit from a list or card and you can practice quoting the answer on the flip side or they can confirm your checklist patter is correct by following your spoken words from the written checklist. Try to involve them if possible. If you don't have a partner, no problem but we recommend not actively trying to find a partner during your course. You will be too busy! There is plenty of time for that later.

✈ **A keen interest in all things aviation and the Military.** Learn what you can. Fly before pilot's course if you can. However be prepared to 'unlearn' some of what you have previously been taught. The Military have very specific ways of doing things, especially when it comes to flying. Often, these methods have been refined after many years of flying and tactical experience, some involving lessons from incidents or even accidents. They do things a certain way for a reason and it works.

✈ **Get and stay fit.** You know what they say, 'Healthy body, healthy mind'.

✈ **Expect a busy social life.** Your people skills will be tested. You will enroll in a course with a bunch of young men and women and you will be expected to work very closely with them sometimes under moderate levels of stress. You will need to be tolerant, not easily offended and easy to get along with. There is no place for loners who regard the whole exercise as a competition. Getting through pilot's course is a team effort in many ways. You will live, work and play with the rest of your pilot's course, so be ready to integrate. Most of them will become life long friends.

WORKLOAD

Nothing is free. You need to be prepared to work, possibly harder and for longer than you have ever worked before. Don't forget, however, you'll be doing some pretty fun stuff too and getting paid for it. Most of the required study is not particularly difficult, but pretty much 100% of it must be understood with a significant element committed to long term memory. The first 6 weeks at both Basic Flying Training School (BFTS) and Advanced Flying Training School AFTS are groundschool lectures. The workload is high during this period as the information is 'fire-hosed' at you at a great rate of knots. Groundschool will provide most of the aircraft specific information (how each system on the aircraft works and how they relate to each other) and numerous other aviation specific topics.

<u>Here is a Hot Tip</u>

It is normal that you will be posted straight onto pilot's course either immediately or very soon after completing your officer training. Normally you will have completed your Combat Survival training at this point. Here is some information that you should consider during your officer training.

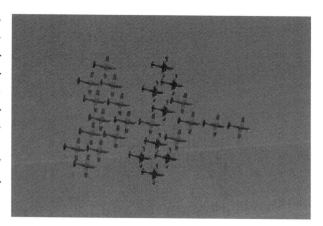

By now you should know what aircraft is used as the basic Military trainer. Was it the same aircraft used in the FSP? If so, make sure that you keep or request a copy of at least a Aircraft Flight Manual (AFM) or Student Air Training Guide (SATG) for that aircraft.

The AFM is a detailed description of the aircraft written by the manufacturer (more about this later). The SATG gives a detailed description of ground and airborne sequences. If the aircraft used in your basic training is not the one used at your FSP or you had no FSP then find someone who has had exposure or is about to start pilot training on this aircraft and try to get a copy of some documents from them. Whilst you won't be expected to know it, if you have done some reading before you go onto pilot's course it certainly won't do any harm. Be careful that it doesn't consume your time whilst on officer training as that should be your primary focus. Talk to others as they may have some useful information about the challenge that lies ahead. Beware of false rumours though and don't get carried away like learning all of the start checks or something like that as it may have changed and you may have to unlearn it.

BHE recommend that you just casually read at least the AFM or the SATG during your officer training. Don't try to learn it, but by the time you start pilot's course you will have some idea of what lies ahead. But stay ahead of the officer training course. You must pass this course first.

We will now move on and assume that you have passed your officer induction training in whatever service that may be. Now lets take a closer look at a Military pilot's course.

AVIATION PHYSIOLOGICAL TRAINING

Sometime before you start flying you will attend an Aviation Medicine (AVMED) course covering the physiological aspects of Military aviation. The AVMED course normally consists of significant aviation related groundschool and hypoxia training in a hyperbaric chamber. You will normally also do a form of disorientation training, being exposed to night vision goggles limitations and possibly be required to undergo aircrew centrifuge profiles to check your tolerance for G forces. All of this training is very important as it may save your life one day. It is required to be completed periodically normally once every 3 years or so. You will learn, amongst other important topics, about the atmosphere, ejection seats, human physiological limitations, illusions and your own individual symptoms of hypoxia (dangerously low oxygen levels within your body). The hyperbaric chamber runs simulate the high altitude, low oxygen environment and help you recognize your personal symptoms if you are starting to suffer from the effects of hypoxia. Take these lessons with you. Hypoxia is insidious. You may never realize what is going on until too late. As it affects the brain and, in turn, affects its ability to self analyze. If left unchecked, hypoxia can lead to unconsciousness and even death. There are many recorded incidents of aircraft being lost and people losing their lives due to hypoxia. This is what happened to golfer Payne Stewart's aircraft as well as a Greek 737 that crashed near Athens with the loss of all on board. The AVMED course is enlightening and is essential learning as it demonstrates your physiological limitations whilst operating in the airborne environment.

CHAPTER 4
Military Pilot's Course Synopsis

T he aim of a Military pilot's course is:

'To prepare you with the skills and attitudes required for further training in single Service pilot training continuums.'

What this means is that successful completion of a Military pilot's course shows that you have the attitude, hands and feet skills and mental capacity to enroll and learn at the required rate to convert to an operational Military aircraft, be it fast jets, rotary wing or airlift. The awarding of your set of WINGS are indeed your 'fun ticket' to fly an exciting array of Military hardware. It is a significant achievement and one you should be proud to own.

GENERAL PHILOSOPHY

So just why is the Military pilot's course one of the toughest training programs on the planet? Most people can be taught to fly, *eventually*. However with limited and expensive resources, you must reach specific competency levels enroute to your wings in a short space of time. It is this time pressure, the continuous required level of learning and rate of required improvement that combine to make the course very challenging. A graph of required learning versus time would look something like this:

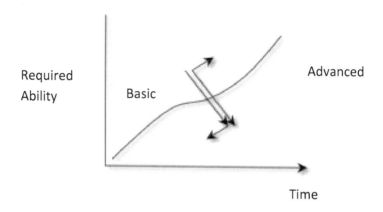

As you can see, there is basically no plateau period. Flying skills must be mastered in a short period of time if you are to progress at the required rate. The next sortie (flying mission) in the syllabus will bring with it new sequences and new challenges that build on techniques previously taught with very little time for consolidation. Anything taught will be assumed knowledge in the future. This rate of learning must be able to be demonstrated throughout the entire duration of pilot's course. This is not only monitored and assessed on every flight and simulator, but also checked at specific intervals by undergoing flying tests and ground based examinations, some of which require a pass mark of 100%. Satisfactory results in these tests are an indicator that the individual can cope with the workload and learning curve associated with any operational aircraft. More than anything, pilot's course is about your ability to learn. As mentioned, the ultimate aim of pilot's course is to prepare you for any operational aircraft conversion on posting from the Advanced Flying Training School (AFTS) with your newly acquired set of Wings. Your next aircraft could be for instance a 4 engine Boeing C17 Globemaster heavy transport jet, the EADS KC-30 A330 MRTT (Air to Air Refuelling), any rotary wing aircraft or a Hawk 127 Lead-In Fighter, hopefully culminating in a fast jet front line fighter Operational conversion shortly thereafter.

GENERAL SYNOPSIS OF THE COURSE

Your pilot's course will normally run for about a year, maybe a little longer. Initially, you will typically spend about 3-4 months or so at a Basic Flying

Training School (BFTS) where you will fly a basic air trainer (normally single engine piston). Successful graduation from there will see you relocated to the Advanced Flying Training School (AFTS) where you will fly the more advanced Military trainer (normally a Military turbo prop or light jet). This advanced course normally takes about 9-10 months. Throughout your pilot's course, you will learn to fly but you will also learn aviation related groundschool subjects such as:

- ✈ Aerodynamics
- ✈ Aircraft Systems (engines, airframes and avionics)
- ✈ Airmanship
- ✈ Air Traffic Control
- ✈ Cockpit Systems and checklist procedures
- ✈ Flying Administration (Orders and publications)
- ✈ Crew Resource Management (Safe management of assets and personnel)
- ✈ Meteorology
- ✈ Morse Code
- ✈ Navigation
- ✈ Physical Training
- ✈ Study Skills

Flying training commences after approximately 6 weeks of groundschool and it will be expected that all cockpit checklists will be known from memory before the first flight. This will require a lot of preparation and repetition. Some Military organizations allow checklists to be read but these will be for checks on the ground only and airborne checks including Emergency procedures will need to be recalled flawlessly from memory. Flying Training at BFTS is normally divided into two flying phases, basic and advanced, where the total flying element will normally be around 100 hours of flying. The flying syllabus includes training in General (day) Flying (GF), Instrument Flying (IF), Night Flying (NF), Formation (FORM), and Navigation (NAV). Throughout the pilot's course, you will conduct groundschool lessons which will be inserted at the relevant time (such as Military Instrument flying technique when you are due to start IF), so even if you don't fly, your day will be busy.

Both BFTS and AFTS units are normally led by a Commanding Officer of nominally Wing Commander, Lt Colonel or Colonel rank. It will have a Chief Flying Instructor (CFI) and at least three Flight Commanders who will be responsible for a cadre of Instructors and students. All of these executives are normally active QFI's (Qualified Flying Instructors). As well as the executive staff, the flying school will comprise any number of QFI's (could be from 10 to over 100 but is normally about 50) and support services staff (administration, education, psychological services and supply section). The unit is effectively divided into three flights. A or B flight is responsible for a pilot's course as there are normally courses that are staggered but run concurrently. A normal system is that even numbered courses are allocated to B flight (like 172 pilot's course) and odd numbers to A flight (such as 173 pilot's course). Each flight has QFI's who will teach the course allocated to that flight. The remaining flight is normally C flight which is the Standardization Flight. This flight is responsible for unit public display flying, Instructor training and flying standards to ensure that the training each student receives is of the highest caliber, consistent and standardized across the entire unit.

MEANING OF ABBREVIATIONS

The Military are notorious for using acronyms to simply terms. We will explain some of the terms used briefly right now.

GF = General Flying   Sequences flown include basic aircraft handling (straight and level, turning, climbing, descending flight or a combination of), all types circuits, practice forced landings from various positions and aircraft energy states, spins, stalls, aerobatics (loop, barrel roll, aileron roll,   slow   roll, roll off the top (or Immelman), derry turn, stall turn + more) and emergency handling.

IF = Instrument Flying   Sequences flown include basic aircraft handling with reference to instruments only (straight and level, turning, climbing, descending flight or a combination of), interception and maintenance of NDB bearings, VOR radials and DME arcs, co-ordination exercises, unusual attitude recoveries, flying straight-in and circling instrument approaches including NDB, VOR, and ILS.

NF = Night Flying   Sequences include basic aircraft handling at night (ie. as above) and instrument approaches and circuit operations. No aerobatics, stalling or spinning is flown.

NAV = Navigation   Students at BFTS start off with medium level visual navigation flown up to 10000 feet. Included in this are methods for determining your position using the Clock-Map-Ground technique, called 'fixing'. Once medium level has been mastered, the students progress to low level visual navigation at 500' above ground level (AGL). The students   are given specific routes and prepare all their own maps from map templates taking into account local winds. From a given start point they must fly the route on the map, including en-route diversions, and achieve the target point within an allowable time limit of normally +/- 15 seconds. Next is medium level Instrument Flight Rules Nav, where the sortie could be flown safely in cloud with perhaps sole reference to instruments with an instrument approach required at the destination.

FORM = Formation   Formation starts as 2 ship, where students are taught to fly in close formation to another aircraft whilst flying straight and level, turning (at up to 90 degrees angle of bank and 3G), climbing and descending, or a combination of the above whilst staying in a series of set positions (and changing between them) at a distance from the other aircraft of approximately 5 metres lateral and 15 metres direct line from the other pilot.

A lot of these terms may seem like gobbledegook to you now but you will learn them on course in good time.

METHODS OF INSTRUCTION

The overall instructional strategy utilized on pilot's course is designed to equip you with the required knowledge and practiced hands and feet skills prior to applying these skills in the airborne environment. This is achieved using a combination of ground and airborne instruction. Training aids utilized are ground training subjects (GTS) given in the classroom, Cockpit Procedural Trainers (CPTs), Part Task Trainers (PTTs), tutorials (TUTEs) and/or simulators (SIMs) prior to flight. Tutorials are used during a block of instruction to consolidate the relevant knowledge usually after initial exposure to the sequence in the air.

Prior to each airborne sequence, a specific ground based instructional lecture is delivered by a QFI. You will be required to pre read the relevant chapters of the Student Air Training Guide (SATG) relating to this topic before the lecture. This lecture is given to the class and it covers the theory of the topic, why and how to fly the sequence in question. The SATG is a manual which contains chapters in detail on all sequences that you will learn throughout your pilot's course. As such it is essential reading and therefore just about all of its content will be committed to memory by the end of the course. More about publications in the next chapter.

COCKPIT PROCEDURAL TRAINER (CPT)

The CPT exercises are programmed, structured events and are conducted in a similar manner to airborne exercises. Each exercise includes a formal pre-flight brief, individual instruction (including remedial extra instruction if necessary) and debriefing. CPT objectives generally precede airborne missions where the same GF sequence will be flown. The CPT allows the QFI to monitor the cadet, freeze a sequence if required, and helps to develop cognitive and muscle memory skills prior to the actual flight. The CPT is also an excellent facility to practice checklists and emergency drills.

PART TASK TRAINER (PTT) AND SIMULATORS (SIM)

The PTT and SIM exercises are conducted in a similar manner to CPT's and airborne exercises. They are practiced in computer based aircraft performance replicas that can be manipulated by both student and instructor. These facilities are normally used to examine and explain instrumentation and procedures before getting to the aircraft. Like the CPT, they can also be 'paused' in mid flight to give time to explain and discuss concepts in more detail or to point out the potential ramifications of errors and why they occurred.

Some Military organizations also have high quality Flight Simulators with excellent visual resolution allowing realistic airborne scenarios to be practiced in the safety of an air conditioned building. These are initially expensive, but are cheaper overall than flying the real aircraft and can be very effective in delivering targeted flying instruction. Missions are also unaffected by adverse weather. Some of the simulators are so real that there is a time limit after conducting a simulator mission before flying the real aircraft, as sometimes there can be a mismatch between what your vestibular senses have detected and what has actually happened to your body. For example, the Simulator may have given you every vestibular and visual indication that you flew upside down but your body didn't actually move from straight and level creating a conflict of perception and 'toppling your internal gyros'. This inner ear balance mechanism called the otolith organ needs time to realign. This mismatch can lead to mild nausea for some students, but often dissipates quickly.

TUTORIALS

Tutorials are usually conducted as a sit down discussion between one instructor and 3-5 students where concepts can be 'fleshed out', questions answered and hopefully understanding enhanced. It also allows you to consolidate in your mind, the concepts, techniques and procedures required for that block of instruction. Staff and student input is essential, however, student discussion of techniques and procedures is encouraged. The aim of the tutorial is to correct any misunderstandings and to elaborate on newly introduced flight-training concepts in a less formal environment.

PRE-FLIGHT BRIEFING

Before each exercise, which could be a flight or CPT/SIM, you will be briefed by your QFI on the exercise objectives, the procedures and techniques to be employed and the method by which the exercise will be assessed. Pre-flight briefs are a checksum of your understanding of the course material learnt so far and relevant to that sortie and usually focus on the nuts and bolts (content) of the flying or other exercise. The QFI will focus not only **what** is to be done, but more importantly, **how** it is to be done. As your flying skills develop, you will be required to conduct certain briefs, such as formation briefings yourself in front of the QFI. You will not fly the sortie and hence waste taxpayer's money if your knowledge is substandard in the pre-flight brief. So you must read the syllabus in advance to know exactly what you will need to know at that time. Your QFI will normally tell you at the end of the debrief what you will be doing in the next 1-2 flights – so you should have no excuse!

THE FLYING SORTIE (MISSION)

The objectives of each flight are clearly detailed in the syllabus. Each flight builds on the knowledge, skills and attitudes required to achieve the course terminal objectives. Your learning will be directed and enhanced by flight briefs and debriefs. It is a building block approach. Once taught, sequences are then assumed knowledge and are expected to be demonstrated on demand. Here is a typical example of the syllabus objectives for GF 1, your very first flight.

GF 1 - Area Familiarisation

- ✈ Perform pre-flight administration and aircraft external inspection.
- ✈ Observe the airborne environment.
- ✈ Perform handover/takeover procedures.
- ✈ Perform 'follow me through' procedures.
- ✈ Conduct effective lookout.
- ✈ Maintain orientation of aircraft with reference to known ground features and attitudes.
- ✈ Recognise training area boundaries and airfield layout.
- ✈ Use the clock code to report sightings of other aircraft.
- ✈ Observe and listen to R/T (Radio Calls).

So as you can see, the information in the syllabus details what the sortie content is. This focuses your study to ensure that you have covered all areas, but more about that later. Don't forget that you will be expected to accurately reproduce this information on the ground and in the air.

DEBRIEFING

After each exercise, you will be debriefed by your instructor. This may be delivered airborne immediately after you have attempted an exercise, but will always occur after every flight in a dedicated debriefing. The debrief will include an accurate assessment of progress, advice on shortcomings, exercises performed well, areas requiring improvement and actions which might be taken to achieve better results. It is best to ensure that you take notes here to minimize the chance of you making the same errors on consecutive flights. Briefs and debriefs normally run for about 30 minutes. This is an essential element of the learning process.

ASSESSMENT

Every dual Military flight on pilot's course will be assessed. A Duty Instructor (DI) monitors student solo flights from the ground and is contactable by radio. His/her job is to specifically monitor student solo flights and also to be available in case of need. As discussed, for each flight there are specific new syllabus items that need to be covered as well as some revision items from previous flights. All sequences covered are recorded on assessment forms and your performance is annotated for each sequence against set and expected performance level matrix. There are various regimes of assessment, but most Military organizations look closely at these three key areas throughout the flight:

✈ **Technique.** Marked in ability to demonstrate sequences with correct and appropriate flying techniques. You are not expected to perform perfectly on your first attempt. There is a matrix of your expected performance level commensurate with your stage on pilot's course (ie later sorties require a higher level of ability to be acceptable).

✈ **Airmanship.** A pilot who demonstrates good airmanship is one that can safely and effectively operate an aircraft on the ground and in the air whilst being aware of the environment around them. Situational awareness is the ability to able to think and fly safely in 3 dimensions whilst being able to project next events. This requires you to have the extra capacity to not only fly the sequences, correctly and accurately, but also the spare brain power to remain within your allocated flying area, follow all clearances, be aware of your fuel state, other aircraft, weather, etc. This is achieved by constant practice and also a good lookout and listenout. Good airmanship is critical to flight safety. Hence it is assessed on every flight. We call it 'Aviate, Navigate, Communicate, Administrate.

✈ **Preparation.** This is the Instructor's determination of the level of preparation the student has undertaken prior to each flight. It is obtained by checking students understanding and knowledge before, during and after the flight.

Each sequence completed in the flight is normally scored out of five. So for example, early in the course for stalling you may only need a level 1 to pass the exercise. Later, level 2 will be required to be recorded to register as 'safe solo'. By the end of the course, now stalling exercises would attract a minimum acceptable score of 4 or 5. The QFI will then provide an individual overall mark for Airmanship, Technique and Preparation where the lowest overall mark is the score for the flight overall (eg: Tech 2, Airmanship 3, Prep 2, the flight score would be 2). A typical scoring regime allocates scores out of 5, which could mean the following:

0 **Fail**

1 **Marginal**

2 **Average**

3 **Above Average**

4 **Highly Proficient**

5 **Elite**

A typical assessment profile is such that if your overall score for a flight is a zero or you score two ones (marginal score) in a two sorties in a row, then subject to previous satisfactory performance you will usually get another attempt your last flight just completed. This is usually preceded by a sit down discussion with a senior instructor about what the problems were and how best to fix them. This tutorial is usually followed by one or two extra flights to perhaps be shown again in perhaps a different way, how to achieve the objectives and to practice your weaker areas. These missions are called remedial sorties. The original flight is then flown again. Another failure may see the student given further remedials or asked to 'Notice to Show Cause' (NSC). This is a formal process where the student is given a chance to formally respond as to why they should not be suspended from pilot's course. This does not mean that you are always only one flight away from suspension from pilot's course. Continuing or not will usually depend heavily on your overall performance on course up to that time and how many extra remedial flights you have already consumed. What you need to bear in mind is that there is strict control over the number of extra missions allowed according to a specified table. There is a finite limit to how many resources are available to each candidate. This has been carefully calculated. Remember it is taxpayer's money. If you cannot improve to the required standard in the time allocated (plus extra sorties you are allowed) then you may well fail this course. These extra sorties generally total about an extra 10% of your total hours you can expect to fly. Remember that graph at the beginning of the chapter. There is no plateau period. The Military can teach a chimp to be a pilot with hundreds of hours, but the key for you is to achieve the standard within the prescribed limit of flights. That way the Military can confidently predict that you can cope with the required learning rate for post graduate operational aircraft conversions. One extra remedial sortie in an FA-18 Hornet for instance is over $50 000 USD!

DOMESTICS

Single members can expect to be accommodated in single accommodation units on the Military base just like officer training. Rooms are of a good standard with more than suitable study facilities. Rooms may be inspected at any time. Students are responsible for the cleanliness, good order and serviceability of all items in their rooms and common areas. The areas of inspection normally include the common room, kitchen area and laundry facilities on the floor. These common areas may also be inspected at any time. The Student's Mess supplies three meals a day and is used as a place to relax and unwind by students throughout course.

The Military base will normally be equipped with all that you need to avoid having to drive off the base to obtain normal services, particularly sporting activities. It will normally have a modern gymnasium, basketball court, squash courts, tennis courts, sports ovals and a swimming pool. The following facilities and amenities may also be provided:

- Base Chapel - For religious services
- Base Cinema - Screening the latest movies
- Defence Forces Banking or financial institution, ATM, etc
- Unisex Hairdresser
- Vehicle Service Centre
- Child Care Centre
- Canteen/ Mini Supermarket
- Bakery
- Post Office
- Tailor

Some bases have far more than this such as Extra Curricular Activities (ECA), like diving, kayaking, camping, climbing clubs, more shopping facilities, social clubs, etc and some contain less. What you see above is fairly typical, but you often won't get too much time to enjoy them all – for now!

Married or Defacto members and their spouses/dependants will normally be housed in nearby married quarters or a Military sponsored home. The houses are generally of a good standard and there is often some choice as to which particular house suits your needs best. Furniture, meals and utilities (such as electricity and internet, etc) will be provided by the member. The Military will pay for all removal expenses and will subsidize your rent. This subsidy varies between nations from 10% to sometimes free service provided housing. The normal range is a subsidy that ensures that you will pay only about 50% of market rent for that location. As well as free medical and dental, this is another perk of the Military. It somewhat compensates for you having limited say in your living location.

TYPICAL DAY

A typical working day on a Military pilot's course consists of:

0600	Reveille – Get up, Ablutions.
0630 - 0715 (living-in students)	Breakfast
0750	Morning Briefing*
0800 – 1650	Groundschool/Flying/Physical Training (PT)
As required	Lunch
1650 (Normally 1500 on Fridays)	Stand-down
1800 - 1845 (living-in students)	Dinner
1900 - 2200 (Monday to Thursday)	Study Period

Weekends are generally free, but significant study must be done to pass the course. As previously mentioned, this is a typical day. Night flying, navigation or deployments will have an effect on the start and finish times of the daily flying program.

* Morning briefing consists of a time hack, Meteorological analysis as well as latest operational status of aircraft and airfields, Navaids, NOTAMS (Notice to airmen), etc. Students can expect a quiz on a pre briefed topic where they will be asked random questions and expected to answer the question from memory in front of their peers and all QFI's and are also required to remain standing if they get the question incorrect.

I can remember that I would normally work as hard as I can during the week getting good sleep if I can. Friday night I would normally unwind at the bar after work for 'barries' or bar snacks and a quiet beer. We would often go out together somewhere and have a social night somewhere. Saturday was my day off. I would surf, go four wheel driving, chill out and read a book, but do something non-flying. Sunday would then be a study day for me.

As mentioned, the first 6 weeks are taken up with groundschool. When flying gets underway, initially you can expect about a flight a day. The daily flying program will be constructed the day before and this details when and who you will fly with. It is obviously subject to change due to weather, aircraft technical issues or personnel who are unfit to fly so therefore can change at the last minute. As the course progresses, you may fly say a dual sortie (with Instructor) and a solo (on your Pat Malone) on the same day - so two sorties a day. So your day will be full, which is why it is important to get good rest.

COURSE HOVEL

A well-formed tradition amongst a few Military organizations, whilst undergoing pilot's course, is to collectively rent a course house or 'hovel'. Some pilot's courses do and some don't. This is a house rented by the pilot's course that can be used as a place to 'crash' on the weekends. It is still positively encouraged as it provides a definite break from the base and its environment and helps to foster course cohesion. It gives you a place and a time to enjoy all the other things that being on a challenging and high tempo course with a bunch of like-minded individuals has to offer. Course houses are at the member's expense and are always in an area that the course-mates like to congregate. A subtle word to the wise at this point. Even though course houses are not officially related to the Military, apply common sense when 'entertaining'. Most cities are surprisingly small when it comes to rent a crowd and the spotlight can really burn.

STUDENT COUNSELLING

The course you are about to embark on is not like any other that you may have experienced previously. Certainly there will be elements of the training that you will recognize and as such you will no doubt address them with your acquired skills. You will not be expected to have the answers to all the difficulties you may encounter during your time at the flying schools. That's where your course mates, your instructors and the training come to bear. In conjunction with your motivation, dedication and strength of spirit, the Student Counsellor can help you work toward the goal of graduating you to achieve your wings. They are trained professionals who have 'seen it all' before and are keen to help you get over the line. So feel free to use them. They are free!

AND FINALLY...

You are about to start on one of the most difficult and longest, high tempo courses you have ever attempted. It will be most probably the biggest challenge in your life so far. You will find all staff friendly and helpful and they will do what they can to get you through pilot's course and make you a Military pilot. Ultimately though, the end result comes down to you. The course involves a lot of effort and dedication on your part, and you will reap the rewards of your own efforts come postings time. You will need to study each night, demonstrating your acquired knowledge the next day in the cockpit or on the ground. It is great fun and you will be able see an immediate quantifiable return on your study from the night before. You will find the course challenging, stimulating and highly rewarding.

CHAPTER 5
Basic Flying Training Program

We will now take a closer look at the content of what sort flying you can expect on pilot's course. Remember that these flights will be interspersed with CPT, Simulators, Tutorials and many groundschool lessons inserted at appropriate points. You will always have something to study for.

BFTS BASIC PHASE

Normally each QFI will have 2 primary and 2 secondary students allocated during each phase. This means that you may fly with 2 or 3 different QFI's during each phase. This is a good thing as often you are shown different ways to achieve the same objective, improving your chance of mastering it as you may respond to some forms of instruction better than others. The QFI's are

periodically evaluated by senior Instructors to ensure that the techniques and procedures they teach are exactly to the same standard, for all students.

As mentioned, pilot's course is completed at BFTS and AFTS. The BFTS splits the training into two phases, basic (phase 1) and advanced (phase 2). In the basic phase you will learn initially GF where you will look at checklist procedures, effect of controls, setting and holding aircraft attitudes (aircraft position reference the horizon), setting different powers and airborne workcycles. You will also become accustomed to the airborne environment, procedures and radio/telephony calls. You will then fly basic aerobatics, low flying, stalling, spinning and emergency handling. During this phase you will also do your first solo! You will then be introduced to IF flying which covers basic instrument interpretation skills and orientation using radio aids (NDB and VOR). This is where you begin to become accustomed to flying without visual reference outside the cockpit and solely using aircraft instruments alone. You will wear a hood over your helmet so that you can basically not see out of the cockpit until you take the hood off which is normally done just before your last landing of the mission. We call this 'flying on the clocks'. Some simulator flying is also conducted, which can provide valuable augmented training as Instrument flying is quite procedural.

There are normally two flying tests during this basic phase and one solo check.

- ✈ **GF Solo.** Students are to be assessed safe solo day GF and display sound airmanship principles. This normally comes up after about 8-10 flights, but you won't get many more to meet the required standard.
- ✈ **GF Proficiency Test (GFPT).** Students are to demonstrate competence in basic general flying skills and the application of sound airmanship techniques.
- ✈ **Instrument Progress Test (IPT).** Students are to demonstrate competence in basic instrument flying skills and the application of sound airmanship techniques.

I will never forget my first solo. It was about my 8th sortie. We had been flying for about 45 minutes in the circuit, when we landed and then my instructor said to me, ok, she's all yours. He got out of the right hand seat did up his straps, unclipped his intercom and opened the canopy and got off the wing. That was it. I was now alone in the aircraft. The seat was empty and I looked at it for about 2-3 seconds to let it sink in, then it was down to business and I slipped into training mode and just followed what I had learnt. I redid my before take off chex and double-checked everything, I reckon about 10 times! I requested a take off clearance, selected full power and that was it, I was airborne – solo. It all happened pretty quickly really. I was too busy to notice the moment. I was just concentrating hard on not making any mistakes and staying safe. I did 3 circuits solo that day and when I shutdown my instructor shook my hand. I felt as though I had taken some big steps to becoming a pilot that day – now I had to get my head back into the books to meet the next challenge!

BFTS ADVANCED PHASE

The first part of this phase involves a revision and consolidation of the skills that you have learnt so far. This doesn't last long! You will then move on be taught more advanced IF such as conducting instrument approaches (NDB, VOR and ILS), Instrument Flight Rules (IFR) procedures and emergency handling. Embedded within the IF missions, you will also conduct NAV training which will include combinations of medium and low level navigation (500 feet AGL) with 'time on target' sorties. This is where you aim to not only identify your target after many turn points, but you must try to be there within 15 sec. You will conduct day/night NAV missions using Navigation aids  and IFR enroute navigation techniques where you learn to fly from point A to B to C in all weather including cloud. Bad weather, alternate airfields, lowest safe altitude considerations and emergency scenarios will be taught and this is an important skill as this is how aircraft will fly normally when transiting from one base to another. Then you will start basic formation (FORM) with equal development of leadership and flying on the wing skills up to solo standard in a pairs formation. This is great fun but hard work! Finally you finish this phase with some more advanced GF culminating in your BHT (Basic Handling Test) where a pass will see you posted to AFTS to fly a more advanced Military trainer, where the challenge continues, but at a faster pace! Here are some more details of typical advanced phase milestones and tests at BFTS.

✈ **Navigation Solo.** Students are to be assessed safe solo day navigation and display sound airmanship principles.

→ **Night Flying Assessment (NF Solo).** Students are to be assessed safe solo for night flying and display sound airmanship principles.

→ **Formation Flying Assessment (FORM Solo).** Students are to be assessed safe solo for formation flying and display sound airmanship principles.

→ **Pilot Navigation Test (PNT).** Students are to demonstrate navigation skills by performing a combination medium/low level NAVEX to safe solo standard and applying sound airmanship principles.

→ **Instrument Handling Test (IHT).** Students must be able to demonstrate instrument flying skills to the BFTS graduation level applying sound captaincy skills and demonstrating good airmanship principles.

→ **Basic Handling Test (BHT).** Students are to demonstrate competency in flying selected combinations of GF sequences as selected by the testing officer. The application of sound airmanship in new and unusual situations must be demonstrated throughout and the performance of documented aircraft emergency procedures is to be faultless.

BFTS SYLLABUS

The following table is a representation of total flying hours broken down by category for a typical BFTS. Some Military organizations place greater emphasis on basic training and others don't, so the hours may vary, but the overall BFTS phase of the pilot's course will cover all of the objectives listed and will take about 3-4 months.

TOTAL FLYING HOURS BY SEQUENCE

Sequence	Dual	Solo	Total
GF	29	8	37
IF	25	0	25

NF	4	0.5	4.5
NAV	22	4	26
FORM	6	1.2	7.2
Total	**86**	**13.7**	**99.7**

BREAKDOWN OF STUDENT FLYING HOURS BY PHASE

Phase	Sequence	Dual	Solo	Total
Basic Phase	GF	21	6	27
	IF	12	0	12
	Total for Phase	**33**	**6**	**39**
Advanced Phase	GF	8	2	10
	IF	13	0	13
	NF	4	0.5	4.5

	NAV	22	4	26
	FORM	6.0	1.2	7.2
	Total for Phase	**53**	**7.7**	**60.7**
Grand Total		**86**	**13.7**	**99.7**

✈ Dual flying involves the student flying under instruction from a QFI.

✈ Students usually log more hours than indicated above due to weather, aircraft technical malfunctions and the occasional requirement for remedial repeat sorties.

✈ At any stage, if a student is assessed as being not able to complete the ground or flying syllabus at the required rate or displays undesirable officer qualities, they can be suspended from training.

A TYPICAL MILITARY BASIC TRAINER

A fairly typical basic Military trainer is a fully aerobatic single engine piston fitted with side by side seats and dual controls. There are numerous platforms utilized by various Military organizations such us the Scottish aviation Bulldog, Cessna types or the popular PAC CT-4B/CT-4E AirTrainer. Checkout our website at http://www.getyourwings.com.au_to view further information regarding the CT4B. There are also pictures of this aircraft including cockpit shots that can be found on the website. See the next page for a CT-4B cockpit photo typical of most single engine piston trainers. You will be given a large photograph of the cockpit to enable you to practice your checks and hand movements. It will also help you to train your brain to know where to look without having to scan around the cockpit for desired information. Before you fly your first sortie you will know the aircraft very well, both inside and out and you will be checked on it daily!

BASIC PERFORMANCE AND CHARACTERISTICS OF THE CT4B:

Manufacturer	Pacific Aerospace Corporation
Role	Two-seat primary trainer
Engine	CT-4B One Teledyne Continental 155kW (210hp) IO-360-HB9
Airframe	2 seat single engine low wing all metal monoplane
Wingspan	Wing Span 7.92m; length 7.06m; height 2.59m
Weight	CT-4B Max takeoff 1203kg (2650lb)
Range	CT-4B Max speed 267km/h (144kt), 75% power cruising speed 260km/h (140kt). Initial rate of climb 1250ft/min. Normal range 1110km (600nm)
Ceiling	18,500ft
Fuel	Useable fuel = 44 Imp Gal (199 litres), Fuel consumption (cruise) = 14 gph (65 litres/hr)
Crew	Normally two seated side by side

The CT-4B or 'Plastic Parrot' holds a special place in many pilots' hearts. It is an airframe that has and is still being utilized for training Australian and New Zealand pilots some 30 years after it was first introduced into service. It is fondly remembered for being both a fun, but challenging little aircraft to fly. Your basic trainer is likely to be the simplest and lowest performance aircraft you are likely to encounter in your Military career, but it is a critical first step. An aircraft like this will be the first Military aircraft you fly solo in. Some of the techniques you learn whilst flying a single engine piston aircraft such as the CT-4B, will underpin your flying skills for the rest of your career. It may not be a rocket-ship, but doubtless you will still find yourself 'hanging onto the stab and flailing in the breeze' at some stage. (Behind the aircraft, feeling like it is all going too fast). This is normal. But with hard work and determination, you should quickly become accustomed to your new 'office'.

CHAPTER 6
Advanced Flying Training Program

The AFTS often runs concurrent courses throughout the year. The course is approximately 37 weeks long, of which the first 6 weeks of the course is groundschool. Therefore the new course starts flying just as the most senior course graduates. This is good news because it means that you will generally always have more senior students who will be able to offer guidance and recall moments when they were challenged on the course and give that advice to you.

Your first 6 weeks of groundschool at AFTS cover topics such as basic engine, airframe, avionics systems, airmanship, aerodynamics and Air Traffic Control procedures. Remember it is most probably at another base from BFTS, so you will have to learn all the local procedures and flying orders. During this time you will also be individually fitted with a 'G' suit, helmet, survival vest and an oxygen mask which are now required as you will be flying a more advanced and capable Military trainer. Flying training commences normally about week 7 and it is expected that all aircraft normal checklist patters be known from memory before your first flight.

AFTS Flying Training is normally divided into three flying phases; the conversion phase, advanced phase and applied phase, with various tests both throughout and at completion of each phase. These phases are a continuation from the flying at BFTS and are numbered accordingly; ie the first phase at AFTS is phase 3 of pilot's course.

GENERAL SYNOPSIS OF THE COURSE

THE CONVERSION PHASE

The Conversion phase normally starts with basic GF skillsets that you will have already mastered on the basic trainer such as climbing, descending, stalling, effect of controls, changing power, etc but now you will be taught on the advanced trainer. You will then do circuits, aiming for first solo in the circuit after about 10 or so hours. The first solo is normally about 1 hours of visual traffic pattern work. Another 4 or 5 GF flights are then scheduled, which are planned to allow you to go Area Solo (fly the Advanced trainer solo in the local training area). You will then embark on approximately 15 IF sorties where you will sit in the rear seat of the aircraft with the outside world covered over by a canvas shroud. All you will be able to see will be your instrument panel. You will even do the take off 'under the hood' which is a challenge, especially with a crosswind. The QFI will sit in the front and take control if required. You will need to pass an Instrument Rating Test (IRT) to progress to the next phase. A typical IRT consists of random Instrument Approaches if they are available in your Military such as Non Directional Beacon (NDB), Instrument Landing System (ILS) and Tactical Air Navigation (TACAN) instrument approaches. The testing officer is looking for the student to fly at the required accuracy standards using correct techniques whilst displaying sound airmanship. During the conversion phase, some night flights are also conducted. On completing the night flights and on passing the IRT, a few more GF sorties will be flown, and then the student will fly a Basic Handling Test (BHT). BHT is a test flown during the day where you will fly circuits, Practice Forced Landings (PFL), aerobatics and possibly stalls, spins, low flying (250 feet above the ground) with a possible simulated emergency to a required standard. A pass in BHT completes Phase 3 or the Conversion phase.

THE ADVANCED PHASE

phase 4, the advanced phase, consists of more advanced gf sorties tackling new sequences such as advanced aerobatics, maximum performance turning, unusual attitude recoveries and manoeuvre of the buffet. you will also fly formation, more night and navigation flying. typically, the navigation starts at high level (18000 feet) and progresses to low level navigation (at 250 feet, 210 and later, 240 knots), which leads into high-low navigation exercises where the student is required to attain a time on target of around +/- 15 seconds. students will be required to pass a navigation test, a formation test and an advanced handling test (aht) in order to progress to the applied phase.

THE APPLIED PHASE

Phase 5, the Applied Phase, commences with some more IF sorties before FIHT (Final Instrument Handling Test). A lot of flying on this test may consist of you being able to fly on the standby AI. The Applied phase also includes more advanced GF emergencies and consolidation of previous sequences, plus limited panel IF (scan with simulated failed AI's), more complicated navigation involving formations and night flights. It needs to be emphasized that not only will you learn new flying skillsets and techniques on course, but the scoring minimum requirement rises a you progress towards Wings test. Basically all sequences by this stage need to be of a very high standard to pass. Your final mission is the GF 'Wings' test, where the student graduates on successfully passing this mission.

The AFTS course is nominally about 130 hours of actual flying but this amount is flexible dependent on student skill, as some students may require slightly more hours to attain the required standard, but this is strictly controlled. Assessment works in exactly the same way as BFTS. At the conclusion of your

AFTS course, a Graduation Parade is held at which a set of Military 'Wings' are presented to each successful candidate, normally by a Star ranking senior reviewing officer. No doubt you will have a definite preference for a particular type of aircraft by the time you graduate. Be mindful that this may vary during course as you discover your strengths and limitations. While your preference is given due consideration, the needs of the service at that time ultimately take precedence. After graduation, postings will occur shortly thereafter, depending on student's individual strengths, abilities, personality, aptitude and QFI recommendations to any operational squadron via a conversion course. This could be rotary wing, fast jet, tactical or strategic transport. Some have even been posted directly to Instructor's course! They are called 'creamies'.

SYLLABUS

The following table shows a typical representational breakdown of student flying hours by phase at AFTS. You will note GF, IF, NF, FORM, NAV and advanced GF (Combos).

Breakdown of Student Flying Hours by Phase

- ✈ Mutual flights are when two students fly together.
- ✈ Students usually log more hours than indicated above due to weather, aircraft unserviceabilities and the occasional requirement for extra remedial missions.

Phase	Sequence	Dual	Solo	Mutual	Total
Conversion Phase	GF	19.2	5.4		24.6
	IF	18.2			18.2
	NF	2.0	1.0		3.0
	Total for Phase	39.4	6.4		45.8
Advanced Phase	GF	10.8	6.0	1.2	18.0
	NF	2.4			2.4
	NAV	17.9	4.3	1.5	23.7

	FORM	14.6	4.8		19.4
	Total for Phase	45.7	15.1	2.7	63.5
Applied Phase	GF	3.6	2.4	1.2	7.2
	IF	3.8		1.4	5.2
	NF	1.5		1.0	2.5
	COMBO	5.8			5.8
	Total for Phase	14.7	2.4	3.6	20.7
Grand Total		99.8	23.9	6.3	130.0

MEANING OF ABBREVIATIONS

The abbreviations are similar in nature to BFTS but are expanded here to demonstrate typical syllabus content.

GF = General Flying during daylight hours. Typical sequences flown here include basic handling of the aircraft (ie. straight and level plus turning and climbing or descending flight), all types of circuits, practice forced landings from various positions and aircraft energy states, max performance handling, spins, stalls and aerobatics (loop, barrel roll, aileron roll, slow roll, roll off the top, derry turn, slow loop, vertical roll, stall turn and more).

IF = Instrument Flying Typical sequences flown here include basic handling

whilst flying in simulated or actual Instrument Meteorological Conditions (IMC). It can consist of straight and level plus turning and climbing or descending flight, interception and maintenance of NDB bearings, VOR/TACAN radials and DME/TACAN arcs, flying straight-in and circling instrument approaches including NDB, VOR (VHF Omnidirectional Range), TACAN and ILS. There will also be unusual attitude recoveries, co-ordination exercises and emergency handling in marginal weather scenarios. The student will be awarded a Military Instrument Rating, on successful completion of the IRT.

NF = Night Flying Sequences flown here include basic handling at night (ie. as above) and instrument approaches to both familiar and un-familiar airfields.

NAV = Navigation At AFTS you will normally start off with high level visual navigation flown up to 18000 feet. Included in this are methods of fixing your position whilst above 8/8ths of cloud or conducting a diversion to the nearest suitable airfield. Once this has been mastered, you will normally progress to low level visual navigation at 250' above ground level (AGL). The students are given specific routes and prepare all their own maps. From a given start point, they must fly the route on the map, including en-route diversions, and achieve the target point within an allowable time limit of +/- 15 seconds. Once this has been practiced they move onto high/low visual and IMC navigation. This involves flying a route above 15000 feet then descending at a certain point (which the student calculates) to fly over a low level start point on the ground at 250' AGL, and then once again find a target at low level with the same time limit. At the end of their navigation phase, students can hack their clock on releasing the brakes on take-off, then fly 40 minutes at F150 and above, descend to 250' AGL, fly another 40 minutes and hit a target within the 15 second time limit, whilst conducting en-route diversions as specified by the Instructor. During navigation flights, typical profiles are that the students fly up to 270 knots or 490kmh at high altitude and fly to achieve a 210 knot ground speed at low level (380 km/h). Here is a simulation in real time: http://www.defencejobs.gov.au/fighterpilot/ - !/pearce/lowlevelnavigation

FORM = Formation During formation the students are taught to fly both close formation and combat formation. Close formation means flying straight and level, or turning (at up to 90 degrees angle of bank and 3G) whilst climbing and descending, or a combination of the above whilst staying in a series of set positions (and changing between them) at a distance from the other aircraft of approximately 3 metres lateral and 10 metres direct line from the other pilot. This could be side by side or slightly staggered called "Echelon" or one aircraft length directly behind the leader called 'Line Astern'. Combat formation is used to follow a lead aircraft at high or low level and allows more aggressive manoeuvring by the lead aircraft. This is conducted at a distance of approximately 700 feet (210 metres). Also taught is the conduct of close formation instrument approaches in IMC simulating flying in cloud potentially landing in close formation landing at the end of the approach. The formation 'pairs' landing is where the two aircraft land together with the same lateral and longitudinal separation as mentioned above. Here is a PC-9 pairs take-off from our YouTube Page:

PC-9 Pairs Take-Off (http://youtu.be/jn3SGPfs14Q)

COMBO = Combination Taught at the very end of pilot's course, the combination flights involve a combination of the above sequences. A student may take-off as part of a formation, conduct initially formation sequences and then the formation splits and the individual aircraft conduct their own GF exercises. One complete, the two aircraft rejoin into formation over a set geographical feature or navigation aid radial and range and then proceed to land together.

A TYPICAL ADVANCED MILITARY TRAINER

We will focus on the Pilatus PC-9, which is one of the most popular advanced Military trainers utilized by numerous militaries around the world. There are many others, such as the Beechcraft T-6 Texan for the USA and the Tucano T-1 for UK aircrew. For PC-9 action shots, including video clips to music visit us online at: www.getyourwings.com.au.

In the meantime here is a cockpit photo of the PC-9.

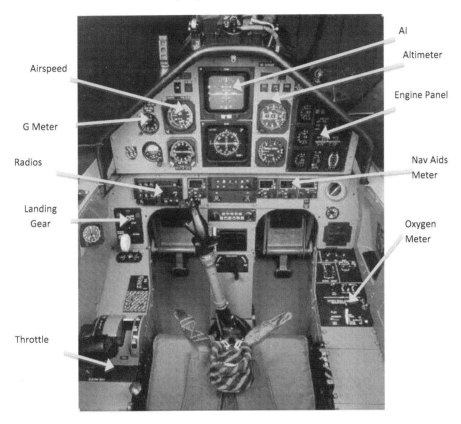

ABOUT THE PC-9

Included here is some background information regarding the aircraft that you may fly at AFTS. It is important that you have some knowledge of the aircraft that you fly at AFTS prior to contacting recruiting as you may receive some questions about the aircraft, to validate your level of interest. Having some knowledge would demonstrate a desire to undertake this training. What is contained in this book would be considered sufficient. What you need to do is research the particular aircraft that you will fly using the PC-9 as a template.

Roles

The PC-9/A was designed by Pilatus Switzerland and has been used for pilot training since the late 80's. The PC-9 is a tandem (one behind the other) two-seat single engine turboprop aircraft.
Advanced Military turboprops such as the PC-9 may also be used for other roles such as Forward Air Controller (FAC) who coordinate air support to troops on the ground. Pilatus aircraft are also utilized for Formation aerobatic demonstration teams such as the Australian 'Roulettes', South African 'Silver Falcons', the Croatian 'Wings of Storm' and a PC-7 team from Switzerland.

Some Basic Specifications and Features:

Manufacturer	Pilatus
Role	Two seat advanced trainer; forward air control and aerobatics displays
Engine	Pratt and Whitney PT6A- 62 turboprop - 950 shaft horsepower
Airframe	Length: 10.18m Height: 3.28m
Wingspan	10.24m
Weight	2, 250 kg basic, 2710kg maximum
Range	1,850km, combat radius 650km, (with two underwing tanks)

Ceiling	25,000 feet
Max Speed	320 knots/ Mach 0.68
Weapons & Systems	Two underwing smoke grenade launchers, TACAN, VOR/ILS, two multi-functional CRT displays
Crew	Pilot, student or observer

TECHNICAL DATA ON THE PC-9

The Engine

The P&W PT6A-62 turbo prop engine is a free turbine engine which is flat rated (from 1150 SHP) to a maximum power of 950 SHP. Maximum Cruise Power (MCP) is 900 SHP. Fuel type is Aviation Turbine Kerosene (F34 with FSII). The engine consists of two independent contra-rotating assemblies: a compressor turbine driving a three stage axial compressor combined with a single stage centrifugal compressor (assembled as a single unit) and a two stage power turbine driving the propeller shaft through a two stage planetary gearbox located on the front of the engine.

Fuel, and therefore power, is controlled by a Power Control Lever (PCL) in the cockpit connected to the engine Fuel Control Unit. Engine parameters are further controlled by an Electronic Limiting Unit (ELU), which ensures torque, inter-turbine temperature (ITT) and gas generator speed (Ng) remain within limits. Propeller speed (Np) is regulated at 2000 RPM by the combined efforts of a constant speed unit and the ELU.

Fuel System

The aircraft fuel system stores fuel in integral wing tanks and delivers filtered fuel to the engine at a rate and pressure in excess of the maximum engine requirement. An aerobatic tank (21 lbs capacity) provides uninterrupted fuel flow to the engine during negative G or inverted flight conditions for the maximum permitted period of 60 sec. The total useable capacity of the system is 535 litres (925 lb). Fuel storage may be increased by installing underwing tanks on the hardpoints on each wing, but this does reduce aircraft performance due to increased drag and airframe G limits.

Hydraulic System

The hydraulic system provides hydraulic power to operate the tricycle landing gear, main gear doors, flaps, air brake and nosewheel steering. The system is powered by an engine driven pump, which is regulated to 3000 psi situated on the accessory gearbox. A separate accumulator and independent emergency system provide for emergency landing gear and flap extension, should the main system fail.

Flight Controls

The aircraft primary flight control surfaces consist of the ailerons, rudder and elevator. The control surfaces are manually operated from a conventional dual cockpit control column and rudder pedal arrangement, with connections to the control surfaces through a system of control rods, bellcranks, cables and levers.

Longitudinal movement of either control column manually operates the elevator. It is statically mass balanced by the use of weights in the elevator horns.

Lateral movement of either control column manually operates the ailerons. Each aileron is statically mass balanced by the use of balance weights bolted to the aileron leading edge beak. Aerodynamic balancing is achieved by the use of sealed hinges.

The rudder is operated by cable from the rudder pedals and is statically mass balanced by weights in the rudder horn. A DC electric trimming system is provided to relieve control forces in all three axes.

The aircraft is fitted with hydraulically operated, electrically controlled split flaps with normal extend and retract and emergency extend only systems. The flaps can be selected to three positions: UP (0 degrees), T/O (23 degrees) and LAND (50 degrees).

Electronic Flight Instrument System (EFIS)

The EFIS visually displays selected flight information in a multicoloured graphical format on the Electronic Attitude and Direction Indicator (EADI) and the Electronic Horizontal Situation Indicator (EHSI). The EFIS has one signal generator, which drives the four multigraphic Display Units. Display imagery is organized so that the front cockpit displays the same as the rear cockpit.

The EADI displays primary flight attitude and secondary directional information. A turn indicator on the bottom of the unit displays turn direction and uncalibrated rate of turn. The EHSI presents heading and radio navigation data depending on the selected mode.

Ejection Seats

The PC-9 is fitted with two Martin Baker Mk AU ejection seats. The seat is a fully automatic, cartridge operated ejection seat, providing for safe escape for most combinations of aircraft altitude, speed, attitude and flight path, within the envelope of zero altitude and 40,000 feet. Ejection is initiated by pulling the seat-firing handle situated between the thighs on the front edge of the seat pan. The parachute pack is fitted with canopy breakers and the seat is ejected through the canopy.

The seat is ejected by the action of gas pressure developed within a telescopic ejection gun when the cartridges are ignited. After ejection, occupant/seat separation and parachute deployment are automatic. A command ejection firing system is fitted enabling the occupant of the rear seat to initiate the ejection sequence for both seats, with the rear seat leaving marginally ahead of the front seat to avoid canopy debris from the front seat ejection.

Other Systems

The aircraft is also fitted with the following systems:

- ✈ 1 combination UHF/VHF radio and 1 dedicated VHF radio
- ✈ ADF, VOR, ILS, and TACAN navigation aids

- ✈ Oxygen system
- ✈ Environmental control system (air conditioning)
- ✈ Angle of attack indexer
- ✈ Standby attitude indicator
- ✈ Accelerometer ('G' meter)
- ✈ Central warning system (including aural warning)
- ✈ Emergency location transmitter (ELT)
- ✈ Crash Data Recorder and Cockpit Voice Recorder

CONCLUSION

The last two chapters may appear daunting when you take a close look at the content of pilot's course. It's like a mountain. It's huge and appears impossible at first. But it is not. It is an incremental process, step-by-step, mission-by-mission, over a long time period. Before long you will look back and you will be amazed how far you have come in such a short period. The key is to keep going up!

Pilot's course is both demanding and highly enjoyable. Most aircrew look back on their time in training with fond memories of the lessons learnt, the friends made and the goals achieved. BFTS and AFTS staff are there to help you pass the course and to develop you into the best pilot you can be in the time available. Do yourself a favour and utilize the resources available at the schools. These two units hold the keys to everything when it comes to forging a flying career in the Military.

CHAPTER **7**

Pilot Study Techniques

W e have said it before and we will say it again. Studying on pilot's course requires effort. You CANNOT bluff your way through and breeze it like perhaps you may have done in the past. Some of the techniques are different from typical Secondary School or University study as pilot's course has a more practical element. You need to ensure that you undergo quality study patterns rather than quantity. It's all about prioritization and time management.

UNDERSTANDING

As you have no doubt already experienced in your school education, understanding a concept means you should never forget it. It is the same on a Military pilot's course. The difference is that within the Military, you can't afford to just quote numbers or text from a book as you will be asked to explain the said concept at some stage. There are many topics including aerodynamics, meteorology, and aircraft systems that build on simple concepts that you already know and are therefore not difficult to understand if you pay attention. Make sure that you don't allow a concept to pass by without questioning if you don't understand it.

Flying techniques can also be thought of in this way. Once you understand what you need to do in order to achieve the aim of the sequence, it should become part of your permanent knowledge (or Long Term Memory - LTM), especially once you have done it a few times to consolidate. For example, when studying for a stall sequence in the aircraft you need to understand that the aim is to recover the stalled aircraft (from a condition where the wing is no longer producing lift) with minimum height loss in order to maximize your chance of avoiding the ground. From your aerodynamics lectures (and high school physics) you will know what conditions cause a wing to 'stall'. Logically, from there, it is only a matter of removing those conditions to 'un-stall' the wing and get it producing lift again. Once lift is being produced, the aircraft is once again controllable and can be manoeuvred away from the ground and the aim of the exercise is achieved. It is the theory that explains the actions involved in the standard stall recovery.

COMMIT TO MEMORY

As previously mentioned, some items must be committed to LTM, which requires much repetition, time and dedication. This is just plain hard work. They must be robustly stored as they will need to be recalled at some stage under time pressure and whilst the brain is doing other tasks such as manipulating controls. Checklists for instance are a good example. They need to become instinctive and flawless. An incorrect check here could result in overspeeding say the landing gear rendering the aircraft unserviceable for many days with increased maintenance costs due to potentially replacing expensive components. Practice them over and over until you don't make mistakes. These practices may number in the 100's, but is dependent upon the individual.

A great tip to help pound this knowledge into your head, is to get someone to ask you to recite random elements of the checklists, maybe even within a certain time limit. Maybe get them to do that whilst the stereo is on. Try to go through the checks whilst jogging or walking where your body is getting moved around like it would be in the real aircraft. If you can get them correct with distractions, you will have a much better chance in the real aircraft. Don't forget, you will be wearing a flying suit, gloves, helmet, Survival life vest, oxygen mask and G Suit (when in the advanced trainer), with the engine running and QFI listening and watching. Don't become a victim of stage-fright – practice with distractions.

In the real aircraft, there will be a requirement to fly within Military accuracy tolerances as well as monitoring radio calls, airspace and air traffic clearances.

Your brain will be pretty full just doing that. You will also need to stay several steps ahead of the aircraft and this requires extra brain space or mental capacity to obtain and maintain an awareness of what is going on around you and what is going to happen next in 3 dimensions. We call this 'Situational Awareness' or SA. Remember this from Chapter 4. It is under these circumstances that you will need to be able to recite the checklists accurately. If you have practiced them with significant distractions, then the checks should just roll out automatically almost and be without error or omission. Not only that, but you want to be able to do this without losing SA and flying out of your training area or trying to land without a clearance. This requires simultaneous thinking and if your head is full just reciting the checklist you are headed for trouble. Practice with distractions, so that checklists only place a small demand on your mental processing power as you will need all that you can muster. Everyone has a different size bucket, which will overflow with water at some point. Extra demands beyond the bucket limit will just not be processed or actioned, they will just flow overboard. You are now at your maximum capacity.

I have lost count of the number of times I have seen a student flying straight and level quite accurately, but when they are required to complete an additional task such as checks or answer a radio call they will climb 400 feet or turn through 30 degrees or both! —it's as if their eyes are closed. They 'see' the error occurring, but it doesn't register. It is not being processed. Another common example is that a very clear radio call is received whilst the student if flying, but there is no response. We call this limited capacity —the bucket is full. The student is struggling to think and fly at the same time, so something has to give. It simply means that the brain is full. Increase your capacity by making the simple and regular procedures more automatic — the only way is sufficient repetition until they are committed to long-term memory.

It also helps to understand why the checks are arranged the way they are. For example, it is logical to start the aircraft then activate the generator. In this way, when the electrical items are switched on, they do not drain the battery. Checklists are painstakingly designed to assist you in operating the aircraft in the most efficient yet safe manner without missing anything. Another example is the engine starting sequence, where an error in checklist order could cause a hot start. If you add fuel then ignition, you will overheat the engine rendering it unserviceable. A typical turbine engine (Pratt and Whitney PT6 for example) costs over $500,000 USD! Another important example is an emergency situation, which could be time critical and preclude the option of referring to a checklist. This is why many of the emergency checks (**Bold Face**) must also be committed to memory and able to be recalled accurately with time pressure. Checks are just an example. Other items such as aircraft limits, radio calls and sequence parameters (such us loop entry speeds and power settings) need to be learnt this way.

I found one of the best ways to study for this was to buy those 4 inch wide white blank index cards from the newsagent and write a question on one side and the answer on the other. I would have one pile for say 'boldface emergency' actions and say another for ATC procedures. I could then test myself or get someone else to test me at any time. I would even shuffle the deck so that I would be required to recall a random emergency or procedure. Pilot's course is not a 'cram and dump' course. You must know all the numbers, facts, figures, rules, etc throughout your whole time at the flying schools, not just for an exam. These cards made it easy for me to revise at any time. Here is an example: What is the boldface for an Engine Fire in the Air? What are the dimensional limits of Training area A? What is the radio call when I want to leave my training area? What is the power setting, entry speed and G for entry into a stall turn?

MUSCLE MEMORY

When it comes to flying techniques, a dual approach of understanding the concepts together with actual hands on practice of the 'stick and rudder' inputs is required. The more the actual flying of the aircraft becomes automatic, the greater the brain capacity you will have to commit to what's next in the mission, and therefore build up essential SA. Muscle memory can be developed on the ground as well as in the air though the use of simulators, CPT's and visualisation techniques (discussed later). Think of driving a car. When you first learn, it takes all your brainpower just to keep control of the car, push the clutch at the right time and change the gears, not to mention keeping it on the road and avoiding other cars. Later, after some practice and experience, it all becomes almost automatic and you can just 'monitor', freeing up valuable brainspace, so that you can conduct an intelligent conversation whilst safely cruising city traffic. This should be your aim with flying: To always have some spare capacity to deal with additional cockpit tasks such as checklists, emergencies, instrument approaches, enroute diversions, etc.

Here is what the start sequence of a PC-9 is like. You will need to know this word perfect from memory and also what to do if it goes wrong! Turboprop start sequence[6]

PUBLICATIONS

Let's go over in more detail some of the manuals that will be your bedtime reading for well over a year. At some stage, you will be required to sign a document to acknowledge that you have read and understood these documents. Some of these we have already touched on so far at BFTS and AFTS chapters.

AIRCRAFT FLIGHT MANUAL (AFM)

This is the bible (or 'duck's guts' as we call it) of the aircraft that you will fly. Normally, the manufacturer of the aircraft writes the AFM. It contains a fairly comprehensive description of the components of the aircraft, from dimensions, propulsion system, hydraulics, landing gear, ejection seats (if fitted), avionics (cockpit electrics), including radios and lighting. There will be sections on normal checklist procedures, emergency checklist procedures, aircraft approved and prohibited manoeuvres, aircraft limitations like speeds, altitudes and G force limits. Also included is performance data like required runway take off and landing distances, climb, cruise, descent performance parameters and fuel range and endurance. It also usually contains a basic section on typical flight profiles, like traffic patterns, instrument approaches and aerobatics as well.

THE STUDENT AIR TRAINING GUIDE (SATG)

The SATG is a unit based, aircraft specific manual that provides a detailed description of all the sequences both on the ground and in the air. So therefore you will have a SATG for your single engine piston trainer at BFTS and another for your Advanced turboprop trainer at AFTS. The SATG is the 'nuts and bolts' how to fly the various sequences (eg. Where to look, what powers to set, how much control input to use, etc). It has been written by the flying instructors at the school and has many years of experience condensed into it. It

---

[6] https://www.youtube.com/watch?v=6o3GKceDv5k

is the primary Military aviation 'how to do it' manual and you should always follow this manual exactly as you will often hear your instructor saying "So what does the book say?" A typical example of the content within the SATG is contained at **Annex A**. It is an extract of the chapter on Basic Aerobatics focusing on the loop.

DEFENCE FORCE INSTRUCTIONS

You will also be required to read and understand various Defence Force Instructions that apply to operating Military aircraft within your country and specifically, operating from that Military base. These come in various forms and take various names. They could be flying Defence Instructions (DI's) and more specific Air Command and Base Standing Instructions, the flying school specific Standing Instructions (SI's), Standard Operating Procedures (SOP), Local Operating Procedures (LOP) and the Flying Order Book (FOB). DI's and SI's are fairly generic and include such details as crew rest requirements, oxygen and medical limitations, air intercept procedures, Military protocols, etc. You will be flying Military aircraft and you will need to know these orders. The good news is that many of them apply to all aircraft, so you may only have to learn some of them once.

The Flying Order Book (FOB)

The FOB is a more formal Defence Force wide publication normally signed by the Defence Force Commander on how he wants his Defence Force to run. It is critical that you are aware of the rules and regulations that exist within that Defence Force. Items include rules regarding live weapons, minimum crewing requirements, medical requirements, operations in adverse weather, authorizing of flights procedures, fuel minimums, etc are contained within this high level document.

Standard Operating Procedures (SOP)

The aircraft specific SOP's relate more to limitations imposed by the local commander. These are very important documents that have often been 'written in blood'. In other words, past errors which have possibly led to accidents, have been reviewed and this has led to a safer way of doing business. This is written down to ensure that all aircrew follow the same rules to enhance standardization and safety. This may include such items as taxi limitations, minimum heights for aerobatics, air space limitations, minimum experience levels for formation leadership, approved and prohibited manoeuvres, ground crew and airborne hand signals and various day/night/Navigation/Formation limitations.

There will also be a numerous lectures on Air Traffic Control procedures, Meteorology and Aerodynamics. As well as the lectures, and before you commence flying, you will be expected to have read and understood the knowledge presented. So there is a lot of reading and comprehension involved.

You will also be simultaneously learning both the Normal and Emergency checklists, which require aircraft systems understanding and a lot of practice! Most of these checklists will need to be recalled word perfect from memory by the time you start flying.

I found the best way to study for checklists was to sit in the Cockpit Procedural Trainer (CPT) mockup or in the actual cockpit so that you can generate some 'muscle memory'. Not only do you know what the next checklist item is but also where it is. You know that you are beginning to get the hang of it when your hand reaches for the switch or lever before you actually remember it. Aircraft systems knowledge was also very helpful – if I understood how the aircraft systems worked, the checklists made a lot more sense and were therefore easier to commit to memory.

That's just the first 6 weeks. You haven't even started flying yet! The same will happen at the Advanced Flying Training school. Some of the orders will be the same but you are flying a different Military aircraft on usually a different base so you can expect that many of the publications will be new and must be assumed knowledge in a short space of time. In addition, groundschool will continue and become integrated with your flying training and inserted at the appropriate point in the syllabus. You need to be prepared to work hard, but when you are doing something as enjoyable as learning to fly Military aircraft, it doesn't feel like work. It is the true definition of how to make learning fun.

Well, how do we cope with all this required knowledge in such a short space of time? We at BHE are here to help. Let's now take a look at how to manage this massive inflow of information and to get it right.

WORKLOAD MANAGEMENT AND PRIORITIZATION

Workload management can be summed up in one word: Prioritization. You will hear that word a lot in your training. Simply put, it means finding out what you need to know now and focusing on that first. We have already said that you will get fire-hosed with information when you first arrive. You will need to manage this volume of information in order to ensure that you do not omit specific and important components altogether by running out of time or focusing on nebulous informationor information that you will not need for 3 weeks. For instance, if tomorrow's flight includes the new elements of a glide circuit, a flapless approach and a hydraulic emergency, it will not be good enough to have only prepared 2 out of the 3 new events because you ran out of time. Whilst you are increasing your required knowledge, you will also be required to pass ground exams in many topics including aerodynamics and aircraft systems for example. You will need to ensure that you know how to prioritize your study to meet the most important element competing for your attention first.

It is assumed that to be on pilot's course, you will already have reasonable time management skills.
This is why they need to be convinced of this at recruiting. In a nutshell, you need to know how much time you have available and then how much time you can afford to spend on each of your topics. Start by writing it down. Write down what you need to know for the next week, rank the list according to priority and then allocate a rough time during the week to study it. Then take 10 minutes to write out a study plan for each night including topics to cover and time allotted for each task. Monitor the time throughout your session and stick to your schedule as much as possible. It may be necessary to re-prioritize your study as you go if you have had a timing blowout. Also be aware that very early on, topics will probably take longer to cover than you think, so factoring

that in will help. As your experience grows, so will your time management skills and your study efficiency. A final tip here is to build in some 'break' time. Chill out every now and then. Grab a coffee, get some fresh air, recharge.

It goes without saying that lack of preparation is severely frowned upon within the Military. As discussed previously, on each flight you will be graded in 3 specific areas: Airmanship, Flying Technique and Preparation. If you have not prepared, your QFI will know very quickly during the pre-flight brief and you may fail that flight without even getting airborne. In return for giving you this expensive and resource intensive training, the Military expects that you will maximize every ounce of training you receive by being very well prepared and doing the work. Another tip is, do not try and get to far ahead. If you are commencing a phase of basic General Flying (GF) flying, it is counter productive to spend hours a day studying well ahead of the curriculum, for, say, formation flying. You may not be coming to that phase for some months. It sounds like common sense but many students tend to try to leap too far ahead enthusiastically without fully cementing their present lessons and to the detriment of current performance. Blue Horizon QFI's recommend…'Shoot the crocodile nearest the boat'. The workload is not impossible and been managed successfully by many people ahead of you. It is this way for a good reason.

Adequate rest is also very important. If you find that you are not getting enough sleep due to studying till midnight or later to keep up, see your Instructor about ways to improve your effective study time. It is unacceptable to be too fatigued to fly due to inefficient study habits. If you are having problems, seek help early. There are many resources available to assist in achieving more effective study patterns. Remember the Military wants you to pass. Ultimately, it is a balance between what you need to know and how much time you have to know it. Again, it is prioritization that is required.

THE SLAM BOOK

As mentioned, some of the study techniques on a Military pilot's course are somewhat different to academic study regime that you may have been used to owing to the more practical nature of the course. BHE recommends a proven study technique undertaken by both us throughout our training and then undertaken by some of our students whilst we have been in the instructional role. Obtain a large blank exercise book or similar and use this somewhat like a diary whilst on course. This 'preparation book' or Slam book, usually forms the core of your study. How you run it and use it (or even if you have one) will be up to you, but a common method is described here. It is generally used to note down lessons from your previous sortie and then the syllabus items for the next event (flight, tutorial, etc). The SATG, AFM, SI's, etc are then consulted and all the important elements for each syllabus item are extracted and put into your own words in the Slam book. Diagrams may help. In our experience as QFI's, candidates who have a Slam book tend to do better on pilot's course, as they seem more organized and better prepared. As a QFI, you can tell if the notes taken during a debrief are transferred to a Slam book and actioned when it comes time to fly the next mission. The Slam book are your personal notes related to your study all contained in the one place.

Let's take a look at how we would use a Slam book for a typical sequence.

So you take a look at your syllabus and in the next day or so, you will do an aerobatic manoeuvre called a loop for the first time in the advanced trainer. From the SATG, you would reread the chapter on Basic Aerobatics and then in your Slam book you might draw a loop and note a typical entry speed of 220 knots, entry power of 45psi torque and that you would apply a maximum of 4G throughout this manoeuvre. Where you are going to look and what will you do with your hands are important. This information will be contained within the SATG and also from your notes obtained from the Mass Brief lecture, which you will have had beforehand. Any applicable limits, related orders or specific parameters could then be annotated in your book as well to ensure they are known for the flight. For instance, there may be a limit that no aerobatic manoeuvres are permitted below 5000 feet above ground level (AGL). This is a fairly typical question that could be asked by your instructor before the mission and it is always good to know the numbers as they must score you in preparation. Another favourite question of the QFI is to ask, 'So what do we need to do before a loop?' If you could answer Pre-Manoeuvre checks and then recite them word perfect, you are well ahead of another student who hasn't bothered to learn them.

This Slam book then becomes the essential knowledge of what you need to know for the next sortie. That way you are not wasting your time on 'fluff' or non essential information for that sortie. Your study is focused and efficient. In addition, the Slam book can be referred back to later for consolidation, especially if you haven't flown that particular sequence for some time. In summary, the Slam book now shows you immediately what the parameters are for the sequence, your weaker points from the last mission, the advice from the QFI about how to fix it and what you did well and why. The best part is that it will all be in your own words. So don't use someone else's as it won't work!

Once the sortie is completed, relaying the important points from the debrief into the Slam book straight away forces you to think about what you have experienced and helps cement lessons learnt that day. It is important that this is done as soon as possible after the flight to ensure it is fresh in the memory, especially if you have two flights in the one day. This is why we recommend that you take notes in your debrief with your QFI. You will already be miles ahead of the student pilot who takes no notes from the debrief, and when it comes time to study forgets half of the points and then makes some of the same errors in the next sortie.

You are diverging quickly on the road to success from a standard student who hasn't prepared efficiently and whose study is sloppy and disjointed. They are constantly tired and are racing down the highway to failure. We have all seen this many times. Your Instructor on course probably still has his/her Slam books from pilot's course and any conversions they did thereafter. Ask to see them if you are still in doubt as to their value.

Tip for young players: Buy a 256 page book or bigger, not a 96 pager as it will fill up in no time! Remember 'Today's debrief is tomorrows sortie'. An indication of what a Slam book entry could look like for a typical sortie (again, a loop sequence only) is at **Annex B**.

VISUALIZATION (CHAIR FLYING)

One of the best ways to ensure the techniques and procedures are clear in your mind before the sortie, is to visualize yourself actually flying the mission. Once your Slam book preparation has been completed and appropriate study of the required parameters met to a satisfactory level, it is time to 'Chair Fly' the mission or an element of it. The actual process involves sitting down in a chair in your room or normal study location, possibly even surrounded by a cardboard cut-out of the cockpit (normally provided on pilot's course), using say a tennis racquet as your control column and say a ruler as your throttle and pretending to fly the aircraft. It sounds silly, but it will increase your muscle memory and help to streamline your thought processes. This is called 'chair flying' and is a very powerful preparation tool. The same thing can be achieved in a simulator or CPT but this is not always available and don't forget, there might be 100 students and 5 CPT. Let's spend some time on it - it will be worth it. Remember this - **Rarely does a good chair flyer fail pilot's course.**

When you sit in the chair, you need to think through all the actions required (eg. checklist items, where your eyes are looking and both rate and displacement of hands and feet to simulate control column inputs) for a particular phase of flight. For instance, in an advanced turboprop trainer when a high power is set from a low power, significant right rudder may be required to maintain the aircraft on the same heading as the torque effect will yaw the aircraft to the left significantly. Additionally, there will be a strong nose pitch up tendency. So when setting a high power on your simulated throttle, practice moving your right foot forward about 3-4 inches and apply some forward pressure on the ruler to prevent unwanted pitch up at the same time as you move the throttle forward. Otherwise you will be a passenger whilst the aircraft does its own thing and you will be suddenly off desired heading and climbing. Also think about where your eyes will be looking to find all the appropriate information like torque gauge, aircraft attitude out the front in relation to the horizon, skid ball, heading, altimeter, etc. The sooner this becomes natural and instinctive, the easier it will be to hold a heading and height when changing powers. The reciprocal is the case for power reduction. If you can practice say just this action of setting powers and what you hands and feet will be doing numerous times on the ground, then you will be freeing up brain power for other cockpit tasks of which there will be many. There are numerous other examples where chair flying is invaluable such as airborne checklists, workcycles (more about this later), radio calls, changing configuration such as selecting gear and flap, overshoots, etc.

Once you are satisfied with the techniques required for your next new sequence (in this case the loop), then you can chair fly to re-practice your identified weaker areas from your last mission. An example could be, a poorly flown departure. Once you have focused on your weaker points, it will be time to string the whole sortie together in the chair. So 'fly' the mission from start to shutdown incorporating all the actions, all the sequences and all the radio calls - everything that the flight entails. Think and act it. Practice where to look, what your hands and feet need to do, what is next, say your checklist actions, etc, so that by the time you actually fly it, you have rehearsed it several times over. This is a particularly effective experiential learning technique, not only before you fly a sequence for the first time, but also to target identified weaknesses once you have already flown the sequence. (Do try to keep the engine sounds to a minimum though!).

Another hint, with respect to visualisation, is to not always visualize the 'perfect sequence'. Remember to think about the 'what ifs'. For example, when chair flying a circuit to land, you should also practice what you would do (control column inputs and throttle movements) and where to look to correct, if you noticed say an altimeter reading 200 feet low or 20 knots slow on the airspeed indicator. Military flying accuracy limits are high and this sort of error would expect to be corrected immediately. In this case chair flying is very useful, as you are not always going to be flying the exact numbers. In your chair you will need to pull back slightly on the stick and apply a small amount of power using the throttle and a small amount of right rudder to balance and maintain your heading. So you will need to reselect a new attitude, hold that attitude and trim away the forces. You would then check your Torque gauge for power setting, check altitude and speed and look back at your adjusted new attitude out the front. By chair flying you get to practice how much displacement is actually needed to achieve the required parameters, which becomes easier as your experience on the real aircraft increases. Remember also to continue with your 'workcycles' whilst making the corrections so that you don't end up having to make another correction because you overcorrected. An example of a GF workcycle is Attitude-Lookout-Attitude-Performance (ALAP) where this workcycle effectively tells you where to look for errors, so that you can correct them quickly to prevent larger ones without looking at superfluous or irrelevant instruments. Chair flying is a great way to practice the muscle memory required to make this almost automatic.

133

Let's take a look at practical example of the final approach and how chair flying can help you improve.

To ensure a stable, consistent and safe approach on final approach to land is conducted every time, the following is a typical workcycle that is taught on pilot's course:

Aimpoint   Scan point of intended touchdown - should remain stationary in the canopy.
Centreline   Use aileron to stay on centreline and do not allow the wind to drift the aircraft away.
Airspeed   Accurate speed contol. Be on threshold speed. Slow speed can kill.

This workcycle directs you where to look, so that you are not wasting time scanning nebulous trivia like your heading on final approach to land. Numerous accidents have occurred due pilot fixation on final approach such as staring at the threshold and forgetting to scan speed and then stalling and crashing. This workcycle forces you to cycle through the salient scan parameters. So in this case, the correct technique is to control aimpoint with the stick using pitch up or pitch down and the throttle controls airspeed. So if you are simulating that you are low and slow on the approach, then you would need a small movement of backstick and a small application of power to increase speed whilst looking outside the cockpit and continuing the workcycle. Chair flying a workcycle such as this 50 times before you actually have to do it in the aircraft for real, will automate this process as your eyes will begin to automatically go to the next required parameter to monitor for errors. Early detection of errors will hopefully lead to the brain automatically commanding small control and power inputs to correct those errors without you really having to think about it too hard. This will lead to a more consistent and safe approach on correct airspeed and on centreline at the correct touchdown point. It is the same concept driving a car. Whilst driving we make small automatic corrections to the steering wheel, based on visual inputs almost automatically in order to maintain your lane without actually looking at the steering wheel and thinking about it too much. In an aircraft though, you are in 3 dimensions and doing about 180kmh as you are about to land!

Another important element already mentioned regarding chair flying is to re-fly the previous sortie or some elements of it. What did you do well and why? What did you do poorly and why? If you can't fly the entire next days sortie, then just chair fly your weaker areas and the new stuff. But persevere with it as it is by far the best form of practice you can do - you are thinking, looking and feeling the flight before it actually happens. Initially, it will take some time to become used to this form of preparation, as it will be easy to become distracted and flying the chair requires a high degree of concentration. So consequently it is fatiguing. So factor this in to your study regime.

Years of research has proven that the best method of learning action skills is via 'experiential' learning, where you actually get to experience the concepts and actions whilst you are learning. Imagine trying to be a great basketball player by watching basketball videos and reading books. You have to get out and practice with a ball! No matter how many great books you read about it, you will never be able to fly in formation with another aircraft unless you actually do it. Whilst the classroom and private study provide you with the aviation knowledge, it must be put into action airborne and practicing these experiences on the ground is one helpful way of getting it together on the day in the air. This method will help you convert data to practical skills and form appropriate habit patterns. Summing up then, visualising the flight before you actually fly it has many benefits:

→ You get to practice the whole sortie before you fly it (everyone does better if you 'fly' every sortie at least once!). By the time you actually fly a new sequence, you should not only know the parameters, but will also have chair flown it many times – reinforcing muscle memory.

→ You logically come across and practice for situations or scenarios that words in a book can't prepare you for, like an airborne runway change for instance or allocation of an alternative flying area.

→ You get to practice correcting errors and recognizing problems/mistakes before you make them or before they become big ones. By practicing the workcycles on the ground, this helps in 'early detection' of errors, so that only small corrections are needed.

135

✈ You get to target weaker areas repetitively before your next assessed flight.

✈ It allows you to think about what you would do in contingency situations in your '1G armchair', rather than a hot and noisy cockpit being bounced around. It helps with the 'what ifs'. Chair flying always has a 'pause button' to allow time to think - the real thing does not!

✈ You imbue in yourself an effective preparation strategy that you will use throughout your flying career and your personal life. Visualization is essentially about thinking a problem through from start to finish with a predictable outcome.

How Preparation is Scored

Your friendly QFI will be required to grade you on your level of preparation. Here is a typical word picture profile that a QFI will use in assessing and grading your level of preparation for each sortie. A range of scores may be given, but typically in the Military, the score ranges from a zero to a five. Five is an excellent score and a zero is a fail. It also gives a good indication of the character traits the Military is looking for.

FIVE
- ✈ Enthusiastic, self-assured and decisive.
- ✈ Openly committed to developing captaincy qualities.
- ✈ Excellent knowledge and understanding.
- ✈ Show initiative and curiosity. Had obviously related points from previous sorties.
- ✈ Minor gaps only.

ZERO
- ✈ Ill prepared in most ways.
- ✈ Failed to read or did not understand the appropriate information.
- ✈ Passive, easily overawed, timid and hesitant.
- ✈ Low enthusiasm evident.

+ Lacks curiosity.
+ Almost entirely relies on rote learning.
+ Little or no understanding.
+ Poor captaincy material.

THE SATG

Now it is time to take a look at a typical new flying event and how we convert the words on a page to a co-ordinated airborne manouevre. The example we will use is flying the loop. At **Annex A** is an extract from the chapter in the SATG relating to basic aerobatics, focusing on the loop. A pre-requisite before this flight is that you will have conducted the SATG groundschool given by the QFI. Before this you will have already read the chapter. The groundschool cements the required knowledge from your reading, hopefully fills any gaps and allows you to ask intelligent questions.

Annex B is an example of a typical Slam book entry in preparation for the sortie where you will fly the loop for the first time in a PC-9. Now you have all of the tools that you need to fully prepare for your next sortie and now we will show you how to actually fly the mission to the best of your ability in the next chapter.

Annex A to Chapter 7 Pilot Study Techniques

PC-9 BASIC AEROBATICS EXTRACT FROM SATG

Aim

To explain:

    a. Procedures and techniques to fly basic aerobatic manoeuvres in the PC-9.

Considerations

Aerobatics are a valuable aid in teaching a pilot to confidently and smoothly fly an aircraft to its performance limits by improving overall aircraft handling and coordination skills.

Manoeuvre Limitations

Flight Manual and Standing Instructions. Section 5 of the Aircraft Flight Manual and Base Standing Instructions detail the PC-9 prohibited manoeuvres, operational restrictions (spinning with landing gear down for example), and the engine and airframe limitations. These limitations must be known and applied at all times.

Aircraft overspeed or overstress. In the event that the aircraft structural limits are exceeded, the aircraft should be recovered to a safe flight regime for the configuration as soon as possible above 5000 feet above ground level and the aircraft landed when practicable using the procedures as detailed in the Standard Operating Procedures (SOP).

Altimetry. As your skill develops, take notice of the height recovery from various attitudes. At a later time this will be valuable information to construct an Aerobatics Sequence incorporating a not below base height. For dual missions, all aerobatics are to be done no lower than 5000 feet AGL.

Lookout

For manoeuvres that require considerable height to complete (the loop for example) the area above the aircraft must be cleared visually prior to pulling up into the manoeuvre. A loop can use up to 2000 feet above entry height to complete. This area must be clear.

Basic Aerobatics

The Figure below depicts the dive attitude used to achieve an entry airspeed of 220 kts for aerobatic manoeuvres.

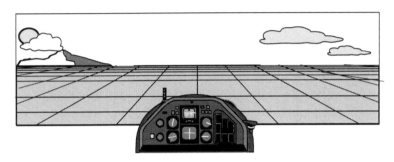

Figure 1. Aerobatic 220 knot dive attitude.

The Loop

A loop is normally entered from a wingover to achieve 220 kts entry speed with power set at 45 psi. During a loop the aircraft is flown wings level, at a constant pitch rate, through 360° in the vertical plane. Positive G is maintained throughout the manoeuvre but the amount of G will vary with the aircraft's position in the manoeuvre. At the top of a loop the aircraft will be approximately 2000 feet above the entry altitude. To fly a loop proceed as follows (refer to Figure 2):

a. Execute a wingover to ensure the area is clear and achieve the entry speed of 220 kts using the attitude reference the horizon as depicted above with the aircraft tracking parallel to a suitable line feature.

b. Approaching 200 kts, visually clear the area above the aircraft.

c. Anticipate the acceleration to achieve 220 kts and as the nose passes the horizon and pitch up wings level using approximately 3 G then cross-refer to the G-meter to set 4 G.

d.   As the nose pitches through the horizon, note the pitch rate and scan to the wing tips to maintain equal spacing reference to the horizon (and therefore wings level) – adjust with aileron if required. As the airspeed reduces, check skidball and maintain balance with right rudder.

e.   The force required to hold the elevator position will reduce but a slight aft movement is required to maintain a constant pitch rate. Assess the pitch rate visually and adjust the control column position (if required) to maintain a constant rate (initially you may just be taught to hold the control column in a constant position).

f.   Approaching the inverted attitude look back over the top of your seat to locate the line feature. As the nose approaches the horizon, ensure the aircraft is wings level and tracking parallel to the line feature - if not make a correction to the angle of bank using aileron (roll towards the line).

g.   As the nose passes through the horizon, use aileron and rudder (to balance) as required to track parallel to the line feature and elevator to maintain a constant pitch rate. As the airspeed increases the elevator control force will rapidly increase and the control column should be adjusted forward slightly (the reverse of the movement in the first half of the loop).

h.   In the last quarter of the loop scan from the attitude to the airspeed to exit the loop at 220 kts. The rate of acceleration should closely match the pitch rate to the horizon. If you assess the aircraft will be slow, reduce the G (and therefore pitch rate) to allow the aircraft to accelerate. Conversely, if you assess the aircraft will be fast increase the G (look at the G-meter) to 4 G.

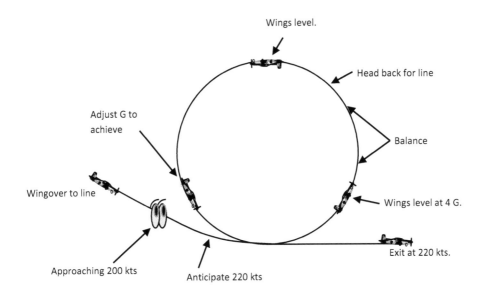

Figure 2. The Loop schematic time line.

Airmanship

Checks. The pre-manoeuvre checks must be completed prior to any aerobatic manoeuvres. Although the Pre-manoeuvre checks are not required between each aerobatic manoeuvre, you must check that height is sufficient prior to committing the aircraft to the next manoeuvre.

Orientation. Continuous aerobatic flying can be disorientating, so regularly check your position in the area. During the lookout prior to each manoeuvre take note of your position. If you are unsure of where you are or which way you are going, establish straight and level flight to re-orientate yourself in the area. To minimize disorientation, attempt to remain over the one line feature for all aerobatics rather than choosing the next line feature that you see.

Aircraft limits. Careless flying, particularly in manoeuvres can easily result in exceeding aircraft limitations and is a very serious breach of airmanship. The

141

G-meter and altimeter should be monitored during aerobatics to ensure the G and minimum height limitations are not exceeded.

Annex B to Chapter 7 Pilot Study Techniques

TYPICAL SLAM BOOK ENTRY FOR LOOP

GF 11   1.2 hours Dual

Last sortie debrief points

- ✈ Start/taxi/take off — Good checks, sloppy attitude control in climb, so climbed too fast.
- ✈ Departure — Not enough lookout, not fully trimmed, see point above.
- ✈ Stall — Forgot for pre-manoeuvre chex. Bad airmanship, DON'T FORGET!
- ✈ Wingover — Didn't pull up enough, too much roll, so fast, high G exit.
- ✈ Landing — Flared too late, so hard landing.
- ✈ Lookout — Happy with this, try to see other aircraft before QFI does.

GF 11 Aims

- ✈ Start, taxi, take off — Keep up good checks, ALAP workcycle – don't stop it.
- ✈ Departure — Trim this time! Fly the correct speeds!
- ✈ Steep Turn — Remember good lookout and reduce power on rollout.
- ✈ Stall — Remember pre-manoeuvre checks.
- ✈ Radio — Sound more confident.
- ✈ Landing — Don't fixate on aimpoint, look to far end of runway for flare height.

New Event - LOOP

- ✈ Pre-manoeuvre chex first (fly accurately, don't climb 300 ft!) – keep ALAP scan going

✦ Entry Power 45 psi/Entry Speed 220 kts
✦ Use 4 G – constant pitch rate, not constant stick position, so scan G meter.
✦ Limits: 5000 feet AGL minimum at all times/ 4G (no more than 6 G)

Here is what it looks like

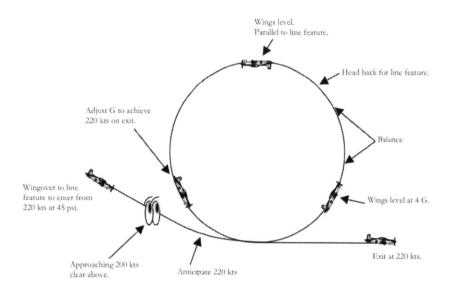

Wings level.
Parallel to line feature.

Head back for line feature.

Adjust G to achieve 220 kts on exit.

Balance

Wingover to line feature to enter from 220 kts at 45 psi.

Wings level at 4 G.

Exit at 220 kts.

Approaching 200 kts clear above.

Anticipate 220 kts

CHAPTER 8
Flying the Sortie

E ach and every sortie including solos can be broken into 3 phases:
   a.   The sortie pre-flight brief.
   b.   The flight.
   c.   The debrief or 'deba'.

SORTIE PRE-FLIGHT BRIEF (MISSION BRIEF)

The Mission Brief is the point at where the Instructor is giving you his/her experience and tips on **how** to fly the sequences and also checking your level of knowledge and preparation before each flight. They will have various training aids at their disposal including Powerpoint Presentations, videos, White Board Mission briefing notes and aircraft models which are one of the most important and useful of the training aids. The structure of the mission brief is normally:

Aim:	To learn how to land the PC-9.	
Considerations:	Wind, configuration, go around.	
Airmanship:	Clearances, finals checks.	
Airex:	Start, taxi, take-off	
	Circuit traffic pattern	
	Normal, flapless and glide circuits	
	Go arounds	
Domestics:	Callsign	Alladin 01
	Park slot	51
	Take off	0910
	IFF Code	3001
	Duration	1.2 hrs

Configuration Dual, No smoke, full fuel, no underwing tanks.

You will need to know all the aspects of each syllabus item in that sortie (Not a problem if you prepared using your Slam book). For example, if a Stall Turn is to be performed in the sortie, you will need to know and be prepared to recite the entry parameters, the specific applicable aircraft limits, the out-of-control recovery actions and the general 'how to fly it' principles – again all should be researched and written down in the Slam book a day or two before.

You will find this information in the SATG, the mass brief, the AFM and all the other information resources you have at hand. The brief is also the last chance to have any minor questions answered before actually flying the sequence. Of course, any major questions like 'What is a stall turn?' would be viewed quite poorly at this time and should have been asked well in advance of the brief to allow suitable preparation time. The sortie pre-flight brief normally lasts between 10 and 30 minutes.

Tip for young players: Don't be late to your briefs and always know your stuff.

THE FLIGHT

Whenever you get into the aircraft, take just a moment to make yourself comfortable in the cockpit. Adjust the seat straps, rudder pedals, air vents, ECS (airconditioning) temperature and ensure your helmet fits well. Ensure that you are comfortable and have a relaxed posture…after all this is going to be your office for a while. The QFI wants to see a well-prepared student who is punctual, motivated, is a good listener and does their best in the air.

Don't expect to be perfect on your first attempt at a new sequence. Everyday is a different challenge; you may be with a different QFI, using a different runway with different wind, weather, etc. So be flexible rather than robotic. Be ready to adapt. Be a sponge and soak up the information directed at you.

The QFI will be impressed if you have noted yesterday's weaker points in the debrief and have made an effort to fix or improve on them in this mission. Alternatively, making the same mistake 2 or 3 sorties in a row, reflects poorly.

Don't worry, the Instructor will know what your weaker points are even if you flew with someone else, as they also do preparation before each sortie by reading your last few flight reports. This arms them with information regarding your weaker points and what they need to fix in their mission with you.

Demonstrations from your QFI are a very valuable component of airborne instruction. They say a picture is worth a thousand words and this is true here. You may be also asked to lightly grip the controls (called 'follow me through') in order for the QFI to demonstrate rate and displacement of stick, rudder and throttle movements required to achieve a manoeuvre (the base turn for instance). You can use these demonstrated examples very effectively in your chair flying.

Try to develop a habit pattern to mentally project ahead; say where will you be in 30 seconds, 2 minutes or 5 minutes. We call this 'next event' thinking to ensure you stay ahead of the aircraft, as opposed to the aircraft ahead of you. This means that you will have thought about the event before you get there. For example, 30 seconds beforehand, you will switch to the new frequency, practice your call in your head and then give the correct call at the correct feature whilst flying accurately. No next event thinking will inevitable lead to flying past the Initial Point ground feature at 400 kmh on the old frequency with no call. By then it is too late. So after your QFI prompts you, you rush, give the wrong call on the incorrect frequency whilst climbing 300 feet. Your QFI will not be happy with this. You are behind the aircraft and need to catch up. This 'next event' thinking will ensure that you do not end up 'flailing in the breeze or hanging off the tailplane'. Thinking ahead is free. Try to form the habit pattern early in your training.

If you feel a little stressed or feel behind the aircraft, carry out the BIBO checks (Breathe In Breathe Out) to start with, and try to relax. In order to regain SA, you first have to realize and accept you have lost it! Remember your voice – don't be a mouse. Sound confident. Be alert and decisive. Enjoy. Smile!

As mentioned, all book authors are QFI. Believe us please when we say that, it is very easily to spot a struggling student. Either they can't manipulate the controls smoothly (lack of coordination), but more often then not their brain becomes full quite quickly. Obvious signs include flying the aircraft sometimes inaccurately and failing to respond to a radio call or giving a radio call and climbing 300 feet. They are looking in the right area and listening but the information is not registering or being processed. They are task saturated or fixating on one task at once. This shows limited capacity. As the training becomes more advanced, your capacity is expected to keep up with the demands placed on it in order to be able to operate the aircraft safely. For example, initially you will just fly straight and level and later your training may progress to being able to fly an instrument approach in poor weather. You must progress and keep up. Capacity issues can lead to unsafe situations quite quickly and hence poor airmanship. This is one of the main reasons that many struggle in the airborne environment. A common example of lack of capacity is the following:

Student turning base to conduct a touch and go in the circuit. (This is something that needs to be mastered before the first solo, which is typically less than 10 hours flying time.).

….student turns base, sets power, lowers nose, sets flaps, very busy trying to hold correct speed, angle of bank and glide path and give the radio call to do a touch and go, Air Traffic Control (ATC) says 'continue' only and gives no clearance to touch and go due to an aircraft already on the runway about to take off. Students reads back continue and whilst fixating on landing on correct speed at the correct point on the runway just past the threshold forgets that no clearance has been obtained and the Qualified Flying Instructor is required to take control and go around to avoid a potential collision. No clearance was obtained from ATC (quite rightly) to touch and go as the aircraft ahead was still on the runway. The student may have seen but did not process the aircraft of the runway despite being told about it and acknowledging it. This is a good example of information received, read back but not properly processed. Task fixation, meant the brain was full manually manipulating controls and correcting small errors and didn't have the capacity to remember that no clearance was obtained with potentially fatal results. In pilot circles, we call this loss of SA. Due to the mechanical task at hand, the student has lost awareness of the 3 dimensional situation they are presently experiencing with potential breakdowns in safety as a consequence. If you could replay this scenario in a full motion simulator and press pause you could demonstrate to the student how, why and when they lost SA in this circumstance. The worst part of this episode is that most of the time the student doesn't know that they have lost it and why the QFI took control. This is what we mean by finite brainspace and capacity. Don't worry, we have given you many techniques and tips within this book about how to best prepare for missions to enhance this SA, like studying with distractions and chair flying to transfer skillsets to the more automated LTM and to enhance overall capacity.

AIRBORNE MILITARY INSTRUCTIONAL TECHNIQUES

The following are some real live examples of Military airborne instruction. It may sound a bit technical initially, but it gives you an insight into the very high standards required of a Military pilot. We have tried to keep the acronyms to a minimum, but this is typically what a cockpit may sound like if the conversation was recorded for various sequences. You will be trained to understand these terms and concepts so don't worry if you don't fully understand them now. We have included these cockpit transcripts here for illustrative purposes, to introduce you to what it is really like.

General Flying

As discussed in previous chapters, GF in Military parlance is basically day flying in good weather. It is where you will start your flying training, initially beginning with the very basic stuff like checklist procedures, radio calls, airspace procedures and effect of controls. Later you will move onto more advanced sequences like circuits, aerobatics, stalling, steep turns, manoeuvring on the buffet, maximum rate turns and spinning. Lets look at example of something quite simple, but can be a challenge to some especially early on in the training – flying straight and level whilst doing checks. One way of teaching a student how to fly straight and level is to have a robotic workcycle that effectively tells you where to look to achieve this task. In Australia, the Military teach the ALAP workcycle. We have already touched on this in chapter 1. We will expand on it here, so that the cockpit transcript will make sense.

Attitude This is what you see when you look out the front of the aircraft and it is used to set a picture with reference to the never moving horizon that corresponds to a desired performance. You saw it in the last chapter as we used a nose low attitude for entry into the loop. Normally we use the flat top of the instrument panel, which is called the instrument combing. So for straight and level flight, we need the instrument combing to be parallel to the horizon, otherwise your heading will change as you have some bank on and you will not be flying straight (constant heading). Let's imagine for simplicity that to remain level at cruise speed, the instrument panel should be on the horizon. If the instrument panel is pitched above the horizon with backstick you will climb and likewise if it is below, you will descend. This needs to be set and maintained accurately or deviations will occur quickly. Therefore you need to look at it regularly, hence why 'Attitude' is in the scan.

Lookout This is where we move our head say from the left wingtip slowly to the front looking for other aircraft, hazards, ground features etc.

Attitude After the lookout your head should be looking at the front, so this is a repeat of step 1 but you are looking for any deviations that may have occurred during your lookout and they should be immediately corrected with pitch (up or down) or roll (aileron left or right).

Performance We confirm correct performance parameters by quickly looking at the instruments to see whether our attitude out the front is appropriate to achieve the desired performance. So we would check the HSI (Horizontal Situation Indicator or Compass) to see if the heading has changed and also the altimeter to see if the aircraft has climbed or descended. If there is an error, then we need to **Select** a new corrected attitude (usually only a very small change), **Hold** that new attitude to give it a chance to work and then **Trim** away the forces using the trimmers on the stick and/or throttle.

So we keep doing this workcycle over and over again until we can consistently hold straight and level flight within fairly demanding accuracy standards. Typically for low experience students, height should be plus or minus 200 feet and heading plus or minus 10 degrees. However, the overall operation of the aircraft is not that easy as you must be able to fly to these accuracy limits whilst achieving cockpit tasks at the same time. Such tasks could include giving a radio call, completing airborne checklist procedures, perhaps briefing an instrument approach via a kneepad chart or even handling an aircraft emergency. You also need to prioritize those tasks competing for your attention as not every task can be completed at the same time.

All of these cockpit tasks place demands on the finite resources of the brain. The brain is not very good at doing simultaneous tasks (try patting your head with one hand and making circles on your stomach with the other, whilst talking to someone and then reverse direction). But the brain can be trained, but only to a degree. You will be far more likely to be able to cope with this normal cockpit workload if you have done a considerable amount of chair flying particularly practicing your ALAP workcycle to make it effective and efficient.

Here is a live cockpit example of task prioritization and how we can train the brain to handle simultaneous tasks. There you are flying straight and level and you start to do your cruise checks and half way through these checks you get a radio call from ATC requesting that you change altitude to avoid traffic. Whilst acknowledging this call, you may also need to stop all other tasks and change heading to stay in your allocated training area. We prioritize in the cockpit by utilizing a Military flying priority rule, which can be summarized as follows:

Aviating: Flying the aircraft, ie level turn at the required speed at 30 degrees of bank.

Navigating: Staying in your training area by navigating back to the middle.

Communicating: Answering the radio call and reading back the correct clearance.

Administrating: Now that the higher priority tasks are completed and we are once again straight and level on a good heading we can continue our cruise checks or lower priority admin tasks such as opening your Instrument Approach chart.

So back to flying straight and level and coping with cockpit tasks. How do we teach it? The key is to teach the student to continue the ALAP workcycle but to break up the cockpit tasks into small parts, to enable the scan to flip between the ALAP workcycle and the checks for instance. This enhances the prospect of maintaining accurate flying standards whilst completing this cockpit task. So to place that into words, it might go something like this even though no words are spoken in the cockpit:

Performance	height 150 feet high, heading good, airspeed 10 knots fast, throttle reduce 2 units.
Attitude	nose too high, climbing, lower nose, hold, trim.
Lookout	eyes left and now to the front.
Attitude	raise nose just little now to stop descent, wings level.
Performance	scan instruments, now back on height, speed reducing, cruise checks, fuel 480 lbs, sufficient and balanced.
Attitude	climbing again, slight left bank, reselect instrument panel on horizon, hold and trim.
Lookout	eyes right and now back to the front.
Attitude	looking good instrument panel on horizon.
Performance parameters in green.	height good, speed good, bank right, bank off, engine
Attitude	looks good.
Lookout	eyes left and now to the front.
Attitude	hasn't moved.
Performance	scan instruments, on height on heading, but DME close to area boundary, so new hdg on hdg bug, lookout and roll, attitude, etc.

So you can see from the commentary that there is little time for rest until these workcycles become automatic and you can now see the value of chair flying. We need to be able to achieve the above for differing cruise speeds, when we lower gear, flap and speedbrake (depends upon your aircraft) and perhaps during turbulence. Some checks like before landing checks have time compression and must be done before you turn base to land. What we have detailed above is a typical descriptive example of actual cockpit thought patterns, which give you a brief snapshot how to fly some basic GF.

The Loop

Now let's take a look at the loop which is a more advanced GF dynamic, aerobatic manoeuvre. We have already chair flown this haven't we? So you have read about it in the SATG, you have received the Mass Brief and you have chair flown it using your Slam book. You have now had the pre-flight brief with your QFI where you have discussed the mission objectives including the loop. Your QFI has showed you using the model aircraft and reinforced where they want you to look and what they want you to do with the controls. Here is what would happen in the cockpit if you were a fly on the canopy listening in.

Now it's time to fly it. So here you are in the training area and your friendly QFI says:

<u>Typical Cockpit Transcript for Loop</u> *(Student words in italics)*

Ok Bloggs now it's time to take a look at a loop. Ok, so what do we need to do before any aerobatics?
Well sir, we need to do the pre-manoeuvre checks.
Good ok, I will fly, you go ahead and do the checks.
Yes, sir, well height is sufficient, 6000 ft which is above the minimum 3000 ft AGL (Above Ground Level), aircraft is clean (flaps up), fuel balanced, no loose articles, harnesses tight and locked, set aerobatic power, mixture full rich, area suitable no buildings, cloud or other aircraft below and now lookout, we are clear left, right, ahead and above, ready for the loop.
OK, very good checks Bloggs especially for only your second time, but what is the minimum altitude for aerobatics in this aircraft?
....ah yes sir, 4000 feet AGL.
Good, ok, power is set, checks are done. Ok Bloggs, I will fly the first loop, I want you to notice how I pull back smoothly on the stick and look at the instrument combing to ensure that my wings are level, we then look at the G meter and set and hold 4 G. Any questions?
No sir.
OK, we will use this straight road just down there as our line feature, can you see it under the left wing?
Yes I can.
Ok, lowering the nose now to obtain our entry speed of 160 knots, follow me through now lightly on the controls.
Following.
Ok approaching 160 knots, lookout, clear left, front, right and now above, speed 160 knots pulling up, combing parallel, G meter 3G now 4G holding, right rudder for balance, eyes back, horizon, wings level with aileron, balance,

line feature, airspeed increasing, left rudder easing back pressure, wings level, airspeed 160, now climb attitude…and now relax on the controls Bloggs.
Relaxing.
That was a loop. Did you enjoy that?
Yes, I did sir. That was awesome.
Good, ok, was the combing parallel to the horizon?
Yes sir.
How did I do this? I did this by pitching up and maintaining wings level with aileron.
What did the G meter read?
3 and then 4 G sir.
That's right. Good what rudder did I need over the top?
Right sir.
Nice one Bloggs, how do you feel?
Good sir.
Ok, let's turn to maintain our area and I will line you up with the same line feature and then you can fly the loop, ok, any questions?
No sir.
Ok, I will do the lookout, so when I give you control, I want you to pull up wings level look at the combing and smoothly set 4G on the G meter. I will talk you through the rest. Any questions before we start?
Yes sir, confirm please we will use that road down there as our line feature?
Yes, that's right, the same one I just used. Ok, power set, now on the line feature, lookout complete, approaching 160 knots, handing over control.
Taking over.
Ok, 160 knots Bloggs, pulling up, combing on horizon, little left aileron, 4 G, right rudder, eyes back, line feature, G for speed, line feature, 160 knots and now climb attitude. Taking over control. Hey Bloggs not bad for your first loop. We only got about 3 G, don't be afraid, otherwise nice work. We have time for one more, would you like to give it another go?
Sure sir.
Ok, this time set 4G and make sure the combing is parallel, otherwise it's all yours. I will not say anything, I just want to fly the loop by yourself. I will set you up on height, on speed on line feature. Ok checks are still good, power set, approaching 160 knots, lookout complete, handing over control,
Taking over........etc.

Here is what it looks like when Mal Bloggs flys it:
CT-4 Loop Sequence
(https://www.youtube.com/watch?v=bzQPUOfZCxA)

Instrument Flying
Instrument Flying or IF is normally conducted where there is a canvas blind or helmet visor which restricts the pilot's vision to only the instrument panel. It is necessary to be able to fly with sole reference to the instruments as this is what it will be like flying at night, in cloud, fog, dust or low visibility. Your most important instrument here will be the Attitude Indicator (AI) which is conveniently located right in front of your eyes. This instrument tells you the attitude of the aircraft (pitch and roll) with reference to an "pictorial horizon" depicted on the instrument. This is why the instrument is in fact sometimes called an Artificial Horizon (AH). If you remember, this was a typical set of questions asked at pilot aptitude testing and included in one of our previous chapters. Further examples of aircraft attitudes can be found in our Pilot Aptitude App:
Pilot Aptitude App ITUNES (https://itunes.apple.com/app/id669233475)
Pilot Aptitude App GOOGLE PLAY
(https://play.google.com/store/apps/details?id=au.com.getyourwings.aptitudetest.v2)

This instrument is so important that often it will have a spare in the cockpit called a Standby AI which will allow you to continue safe flying in the event of

the Main AI failing. Pilots who think that the human vestibular system (balance organs contained in the inner ear) can determine attitude in conditions of zero visibility will be sadly mistaken, often with fatal results. There are numerous examples whereby the human vestibular system will give powerful but directly conflicting signals to that displayed on the instruments.

155

This is due to the vulnerability of the vestibular system where it can be easily tricked. These human senses can provide the pilot with powerful sensations that when enacted via control inputs can often make the situation worse and potentially unrecoverable. An old saying is to believe your instruments provided there are no fail indications, no matter what they may say or what your body is feeling Many of these illusions are documented. Look them up! The somatogravic, somatogyral and the 'Leans' illusions are examples of spatial disorientation that have had fatal outcomes in the past. Your instruments and your scan of the data that they are providing, are critical to maintaining safe, controlled flight.

When flying instruments you will be taught the conventional T scan whereby the AI is the apex of the T with the Airspeed indicator to the left, the altimeter to the right and the HSI or compass underneath the AI. These are the primary instruments that must be scanned very regularly to ensure that they indicate the parameters desired by the pilot. The AI is central to that scan and should be looked at least once every 2 seconds or so. So like GF, an attitude must be set accurately and this is done via a pitch dot and any pitch attitude can be set from zero degrees pitch to 90 degrees nose up or nose down. Typical cruise speed attitude is normally about zero degrees pitch. The correct pitch (attitude) together with the correct power will give you the desired performance.

POWER + ATTITUDE = PERFORMANCE.

So zero pitch plus cruise power equals level flight at the cruise speed. A tiny attitude change of say 2 degrees nose up means the aircraft will now climb and the speed will reduce. This is undesirable. So a very small movement of the pitch dot will result quickly in undesired performance. So it is important to set the desired attitude, hold that attitude and trim…and then check it about every two seconds to ensure that it hasn't moved. Accuracy is very important especially instrument flying and it is very easy as a QFI to see if someone is setting attitudes on the AI and holding it or simply chasing performance. This is where when you are climbing you 'just lower the nose' to start a descent and vise versa. Chasing performance is like a chasing a dog's tail - you never get there. You must have a target attitude in mind, try to set it rather than push/pull by following the VSI.

Another important part of the scan when looking at the AI is not only the pitch but also the fixed wings. For straight flight, the wings must be parallel to the depicted horizon. If they are tilted or not level then the aircraft is banking and the heading will change. The rate of change is directly related to the angle of bank as set on the bank angle pointer. Also, very close by the AI will be the skidball which displays if any yaw (unbalanced rudder) is present. So to hold a constant heading, the wings must be level with the horizon and the skidball must be in the middle. If it is left of centre, then left rudder must be depressed and then the forces trimmed out. So here is a description of a typical instrument workcycle scan:

AI *(Dot, Wings, Pointer, Ball)*, Altimeter, VSI, AI *(Dot Wings, Pointer, Ball)*, ASI, AI, HSI, AI, DME, AI….

This is just for straight and level. There is also turning, climbing, descending and climbing and descending turns with the end result being able to fly instrument approaches to land. To accomplish this, we use additional instruments such as the Course Bar on the HSI and a Glide Slope indicator during ILS (Instrument Landing System) approaches. So the scan needs to include instruments such as these whilst achieving cockpit tasks, such as checks, referring to the instrument approach chart and responding to radio calls. This is a challenge to most pilot trainees and requires a lot of ground based chair flying practice and determination to improve. Strong hand-eye coordination is also required and the ability to quickly and accurately interpret and rank information by importance. Remember the aptitude questions from chapter 2 which effectively asked you to do this. Instrument flying is often an area where students struggle, as it requires significant cognitive ability under time compression in conjunction with coordinated control inputs.

Instrument Approach

Let's take a look at a real, live example of an instructional sequence involving the student learning to do an Instrument Approach. This is a critical aviation skill as it allows the aircraft to be recovered safely to an airfield in the event of bad weather or night operations, but even more importantly it allows the aircrew themselves to recover safely. Unfortunately most wars these days are fought in anything other than broad daylight, such as exclusively night ops say

157

using NVG (Night Vision Goggles). This is a good example of achieving numerous cockpit tasks in order to conduct an instrument approach recovery to an airfield. Initially you will learn in VMC (Visual Meteorological Conditions), which basically means good weather. Then you will progress to flying on instruments, where you will have no reference to the outside world from inside the cockpit due to either an instrument visor or cockpit instrument canvas 'bag'. In effect you are in a sealed enclosed cockpit and we call it 'flying under the bag'. It simulates that you are in cloud where you cannot see anything.

Before we look at this mission more closely it is important to realize that you would have flown 7 or 8 missions like this already, so this would not be your first instrument mission! Ok, so you are in your training area and your syllabus states that you are to recover to base via an Instrument Approach. Let's assume that you have had all the required briefings and that this is the first time that you will have seen an approach in the air. Today we will do an ILS Approach recovery to land.

Righto, it's time to recover.

Typical Cockpit transcript.

Bloggs as we discussed on the ground before we do the approach we need to do the descent and rejoin checks. I want you to fly the aircraft and I will do the checks. Maintain 200 knots and heading 060 degrees at 8000 ft. Any questions? *No sir, 8000 feet, 060 degrees.*
I will brief the approach this time, next mission it will be your turn.
Ok, sir.
This will be an ILS to runway 36, inbound course 001, descent point on glideslope intersection, outer marker check height of 2520 feet at 5.1 miles, decision altitude 210 feet, missed approach runway heading to 5000 feet. Any questions Bloggs?
No sir, understood.
OK, now for the radio call, you fly, I will give the call.
Radar, Aladdin 01, 270 radial, 30 miles, 8000 ft, request radar vectors ILS to base.

Aladdin 01, this is radar, identified, turn right heading 090, descend 5000 feet, expect runway 36.

Right 090, 5000, runway 36, Aladdin 01.

OK Bloggs, start a descent to 5000 feet, maintain 200 knots and heading 090, I have done the checks and we are now ready for the approach. My radio call.

Aladdin 01, ready for approach.

Aladdin 01, radar, cleared ILS runway 36, report established.

ILS 36, wilco, Aladdin 01

Ok Bloggs, look at your DME distance. What does it read?

17 miles, sir.

Good, what radial are we on?

190 radial.

OK, now we need to turn left onto heading 030 to intercept the final. So set 030 on the heading bug and start your turn. That's it roll out now. Now select speedbrake out and set 20 torque on the throttle. Look at your AI, maintain attitude and trim. Good now raise the nose as you slow down and set 2 degrees nose up. Maintain 5000 feet. What's next Bloggs?

The before landing checklist sir, once the speed gets below 150.

Very good, back to your scan. AI, altimeter, VSI, AI, airspeed, AI, course bar, AI, altimeter, VSI, AI, airspeed, now below 150, start your before landing checks now.

Speed below 150, gear down, flap take off, power, 24 torque, AI, altimeter, VSI, AI course bar, it's now moving.

Good turn left onto the heading bug to intercept, my radios.

Aladdin 01, established localizer.

Aladdin 01, radar, contact tower on Stud 2.

Stud 2, Aladdin 01.

Base Tower, Aladdin 01, 12 miles, ILS 36, 3 greens to land.

Aladdin 01, tower, report final approach fix.

Wilco, Aladdin 01.

3 greens, flap take off, fuel 525 above minimum, harness secure, threshold speed 90, before landing checks complete.

Good, glideslope approaching profile, land flap now 3 degrees nose down Bloggs. Flap land, power 20 torque, 3 nose down, 5000 feet for check height 3520 feet. That's it Bloggs, now scan, AI, course bar, glideslope, AI, airspeed, AI, altimeter, AI, course bar, etc.....

There are many variations to how this particular sequence could be taught, but this narrative above is just a snapshot of a typical instrument airborne instructional event. Notice how the QFI has load shed the student and ensured that he has broken down the exercise so that the student is given the core task of flying the approach. In the early stages, many of the periphal tasks will be done by the QFI. Later on as the student gets more practice, they will be expected to handle al of the se periphal tasks, like setup procedures, checks and radio calls.

Formation

Formation Flying or FORM is one of the most enjoyable parts of a pilot's course but can also be one of the most challenging. It begins with a leader briefing the wingman on the mission details, such as callsign, crew composition, mission timings, fuel requirements, expected weather, contents and timings of mission elements, lead change and how the aircraft will recover back to base. Also covered is what procedures are expected if things go wrong such as an emergency or if an aircraft has lost sight of the other. These 'blind' procedures for instance must be immediately followed as now you have two aircraft in a very small patch of airspace that cannot see each other. Other items briefed here could include rejoin procedures, required hand signals, radio calls, expected actions and who will lead the formation home.

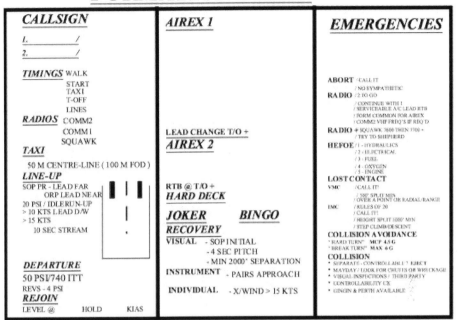

FORMATION BRIEF

CALLSIGN	AIREX 1	EMERGENCIES
1. _____ /		
2. _____ /		
TIMINGS WALK		ABORT /CALL IT
START		/ NO SYMPATHETIC
TAXI		RADIO /2 TO GO
T-OFF		/ CONTINUE WITH 1
LINES		/ SERVICEABLE A/C LEAD RTB
RADIOS COMM2		/ FORM COMMON FOR AIREX
COMM1	LEAD CHANGE T/O +	/ COMM2 VHF FRDQ'S IF REQ'D
SQUAWK	AIREX 2	RADIO + SQUAWK 7600 THEN 7700 +
TAXI		/ TRY TO SHEPHERD
50 M CENTRE-LINE (100 M FOD)		HEFOE /1 - HYDRAULICS
LINE-UP		/2 - ELECTRICAL
SOP PR - LEAD FAR	RTB @ T/O +	/3 - FUEL
ORP LEAD NEAR	HARD DECK	/4 - OXYGEN
20 PSI / IDLE RUN-UP		/5 - ENGINE
> 10 KTS LEAD D/W	JOKER BINGO	LOST CONTACT
> 15 KTS		VMC /CALL IT
10 SEC STREAM	RECOVERY	/ 30° SPLIT MIN
	VISUAL - SOP INITIAL	/ OVER A POINT OR RADIAL/RANGE
	- 4 SEC PITCH	IMC / RULES OF 20
	- MIN 2000' SEPARATION	/ CALL IT!
DEPARTURE	INSTRUMENT - PAIRS APPROACH	/ HEIGHT SPLIT 1000' MIN
50 PSI/740 ITT		/ STEP CLIMB/DESCENT
REVS - 4 PSI	INDIVIDUAL - X/WIND > 15 KTS	COLLISION AVOIDANCE
REJOIN		"HARD TURN" MCP 4.5 G
LEVEL @ HOLD KIAS		"BREAK TURN" MAX 6 G
		COLLISION
		* SEPARATE - CONTROLLABLE ? EJECT
		* MAYDAY / LOOK FOR CHUTES OR WRECKAGE
		* VISUAL INSPECTIONS / THIRD PARTY
		* CONTROLLABILITY CX
		* GINGIN & PERTH AVAILABLE

The formation phase is normally where two aircraft will fly within 3-4 metres of each other. Initially this begins from straight and level working up to being able to maintain position whilst the leader is manoeuvring up to and beyond 90 degrees of bank with rolling and pitching manoeuvres. You will also learn to change position from the left side (echelon left) to the right side (echelon right) via a crossunder manouevre. You will also learn to fly directly behind the leader called line astern. You will learn breakaway procedures where you will turn away from the leader and reverse the turn to be able to rejoin to the left or right whilst the leader is either straight or level or in a constant turn. There are many other objectives in the form phase such as Combat (sort of like aerial dogfighting) and Tactical Formation where the aircraft are maintained about 3000 feet apart and conduct various procedures to maintain station whilst turning and looking out for each other without the high workload of close formation. Formation landings and workups to 3 and 4 ship formation procedures may also be covered. Here is a brief snapshot of a description of what we are looking for when it comes to maintaining position in echelon left as the wingman.

It is important to know firstly that the student will have been specifically briefed on what to look for when flying formation. To fly stable and safe formation requires a series of cues to be maintained in 3 dimensions irrespective of where the horizon is or what the other aircraft is doing. Very little time will be spent looking inside the cockpit. For example when sitting in the cockpit and looking to the right towards the leader a typical cue is to line up say the wingtip navigation light with the exhaust outlet of the engine. This will provide an instant indication to you, the wingman if you are too far forward or back or too high or too low. Secondly you may need to look at the tail of the leader to ensure that you can see straight down the leading edge of the elevator. This will tell you whether you are too close or far away. So by scanning these cues in a regular fashion, a wingman will be looking in the right places to make the necessary control inputs to maintain position. This scan is valid no matter what the leader aircraft is doing, whether it be straight and level of at 90 degrees of bank

Rear Nav light in exhaust duct.

Looking along leading edge of Horizontal Stabilizer.

Echelon Left

Echelon Left Instructional Sequence

So imagine you are the student and I am the Instructor. You are flying Echelon left on the leader who is doing some gentle manoeuvring. I would have briefed you to scan Wingtip (For nav light inside exhaust duct), Tail (Scan leading edge of elevator to ensure you can see along its front edge) and pilot (scan leader for hand signals or head movement to indicate an impending turn). So the scan I want you to do is Tip – Tail – Pilot. Every now and then you will take a photograph with your eyes of the skidball inside the cockpit to ensure you are in balanced flight, as it will make your formation easier.

This scan is maintained throughout until an error is detected. If the aircraft has now fallen back and is perhaps a little low on the leader then this should be easily seen as the cues will no longer line up. Military pilot's are taught to not accept being out of position and you will slowly be expected to deliberately take steps to regain the correct position. To do this, you will fix the height first (up or down), in this case up, so a little bit of backstick is required. Next is forward or back, in this case you have fallen back so you will need to add a little power. How much? Just a small correction or you will overshoot. If you have also drifted wide (check tail cue to confirm), you will need to come in towards the leader with power and right aileron. So the correction workcycle is UP-FORWARD-IN. Then it is back to the scan Tip-Tail-Pilot to see if there are any further errors as you fly gracefully around the sky flying in close formation with your leader.

Hot tips are to rest your right arm on your kneepad to minimize movements of shoulder, elbow and wrist. Great formation flying is done with your fingers only. Your left arm should rest against the left wall of the aircraft with your wrist acting as a swivel to increase or decrease the throttle. A 'free' arm will no doubt over control the throttle making corrections too large in amplitude translating to large oscillations in movement compared to your leader. The key is small movements, rather than large corrections. Quick movements will alarm the leader. You want your aircraft to move about your leader at walking pace. Slow and predictable.

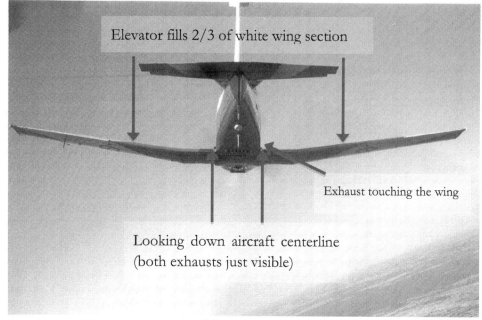

Elevator fills 2/3 of white wing section

Exhaust touching the wing

Looking down aircraft centerline
(both exhausts just visible)

Line Astern

The good thing about this series of scans is that it works no matter what attitude or G the leader is attaining. Constant practice should lead to rapid skill improvement in formation skills particularly if you chair fly the scan, hand signals and sequences. You can even chair fly with your wingman! Below is a pictorial representation of the line astern position. Effectively you will sit one aircraft length behind the leader and slightly low to avoid his wake turbulence.

Here is some cool formation flying. Can you see yourself doing this one day?
Roulettes - Fun in the Sun
(https://www.youtube.com/watch?v=Cp-DmzxSBu8)

Navigation

Now let's place you as a fly on the canopy during a Navigation mission. Obviously we can't cover the entire Nav syllabus in this book or it would be >1000 pages but we are going to describe a narrative as it would typically occur in the airborne teaching environment. This mission would typically occur about half way through the Nav syllabus. Don't worry if you don't follow everything now – it is just to give you an idea. You are flying at 16 000 feet and you have planned your Nav at 240 knots groundspeed. You have just flown past a fix, which is a major river junction. You are 1 mile right of track and checking your watch you are 35 seconds late, you have a turnpoint in 4.5 minutes....

Typical Cockpit transcript.

So Bloggs, how late are you at the fix?
35 seconds sir.
So how will you fix this?
I need to decelerate.
When we are late, we ......
Ah yes, accelerate. Ok, I am 35 seconds late, flying 210 knots indicated to maintain 240 knots groundspeed. I need to add 35 knots for 4 minutes. Time now 31:30, so at 32 minues I will fly 210 + 35 =245 knots indicated until time 36 minutes. Then I will fly a new base speed of 215 knots to avoid the late error re-occuring. I am also 1 mile right of track. My heading now is 230 degrees, my new heading will be 230-15 = 215 degrees, standard closing angle correction for 1 minute. I will also start this correction at time 32. Time now, coming up to 32, turning left and accelerating.
Nice work, Bloggs, look at your altitude, you are climbing whilst you are doing the maths. Make sure that you keep your ALAP workcycle going whilst you are calculating your corrections.
Ok, sir. Next event turn point at 36:30. Map out, pre turn point checks. New track 342 degrees, set on course bar, new heading will be 339 degrees as I will have 3 degrees of drift. Altitude will remain at 16 000 feet, new base speed will be 220 due increased headwind. I should be there at time 36:30. My turnpoint is a major crossroad junction in a valley south west of a large town. Time now 33, re-adjust heading 228. Next event, speed correction at 36 minutes and turn point 30 seconds later. Map away. Fly accurately.

As you can see from this Nav transcript, you need to be able to fly the aircraft accurately whilst you conduct simultaneous cockpit tasks – in this case mental calculations and pre turn point checks. Hopefully you can see the value of pre mission chair flying preparation and it's value in assisting you to perform in the cockpit. At this stage on the course, the actual flying and application of the

ALAP workcycle needs to become basically automatic. You are now utilizing the aircraft to perform Military functions such as simulating a bombing run.

Debrief

Debriefs occur at the end of every flight and cover all aspects of the flight from start to shutdown. The debriefs are very important to consolidate the lessons (good and not so good) that you have just learnt. This is the food that feeds  your Slam book, so don't starve it, as no mission is perfect. It is a vital part of the learning process. Remember, the Instructors are teaching you to be a competent Military pilot capable of undertaking any Military operational conversion. They are not just teaching you to fly the aircraft, but they are using these aircraft as flying platforms to teach you the techniques and habit patterns that you will use for the rest of your aviation career. The lessons you learn on Military pilot's course will be with you when you progress onto an operational aircraft, therefore, get used to ensuring the lessons you learn today, will never be forgotten tomorrow.

Whilst completing a sequence correctly is desired, attention will be drawn to shortcomings in your debrief. Whilst you will be praised for good performance, addressing shortcomings is normal as there is no such thing as the perfect sortie. It is the Instructor's job to pinpoint these **what** errors occurred, **why** they happened and then **how** they can be rectified. In many cases, the debrief can appear quite critical. It is intended to be constructive criticism and not targeted at you personally. The intention is to succinctly identify these shortcomings and to correct them with appropriate advice. A typical student will generally walk away from a sortie with many notes on required improvement areas. For someone who has studied very hard, chair flown extensively and then flown the aircraft the best they can, this perceived criticism day in and day out must be able to be anticipated and then be acted upon in a positive manner. So be ready for it. Remember, the Instructors are not trying to attack **you**, they are trying to make you a better Military pilot. It is as simple as that. A student needs to not just survive on this constructive criticism, but thrive on it. It must be understood that constructive analysis is the quickest and most effective way to learn about a topic that has the potential to be lethal. The QFI would be doing you a disservice to allow errors or omissions to remain unaddressed to make you feel better about yourself or to be your mate, as these could lead to greater problems downstream.

As mentioned, the debrief is not just constructive criticism. It will also highlight the good points of the sortie. Take notice of what it was the Instructor thought was good and why it was good and think how you would apply that to other sequences. Listen and take notes. Even if you don't agree immediately with what has been said, try to take some value from the comments. Don't argue, just do better on the next attempt! The Instructors are trained to teach all sequences and they have often seen them many times, sometimes thousands! They will also have empathy, as they have all been where you are now.

Now you have the data you need to focus your preparation. During your study time, review the debrief notes again. Think about how to implement suggested improvements or how to avoid making the same mistakes again. These points can be added to your Slam book and then practiced in your chair. As your experience level grows, your Instructor will expect you to critique your own performance and extract the lessons in the debrief yourself. They may say, 'So how was this mission?' Once you can see your own strengths and weaknesses in flying, recognize your limitations, assess your own performance and come up with strategies to fix problems or implement solutions, the battle is won! Ultimately, the aim is to prepare you for a time when you don't need an Instructor with you – maybe solo in a fast jet! An honest and comprehensive self generated debrief is a positive step in that direction.

A WORD ON CAPTAINCY

When flying the sortie, the Instructor wants to see you behave as the captain of the aircraft even if you only have a few hours of flying experience. Remember your first solo could be less than 10 hours flying time. A major element of being a captain is being able to make a decision based on the information available at the time and then implementing that decision toward a satisfactory outcome. Don't guess, but be prepared to make positive decisions, sometimes quickly, and don't rely on the QFI to make it for you. Making errors is all part of the learning process, so be prepared to make the decisions. Your QFI will tell you if your decision is flawed.

Avoid 'second-guessing' or trying to do what you think the Instructor wants to hear and see. It wastes too much of your valuable brain space and will probably see you making a mess of whatever it was you were trying to do anyway. The easiest approach is to fly like the Instructor wasn't there. Don't wait for approval for your decisions from the other seat because there may not be time. The QFI will take into account your experience and will let you make all the decisions unless their experience suggests they need to override it. Your instructors will have most probably seen the situation before and won't let you do anthing unsafe. Remember, the Instructors are trying to prepare **YOU** to be a captain and as such, they want to see how **YOU** handle the situations presented and whether **YOU** can operate the aircraft safely and within limits.

Here is an example:

You are on final approach about to land. The tower controller has not cleared you to land yet as there is an aircraft taking off. You are now approaching your minimum altitude where you must Go Around if you have no clearance (normally about 200 feet AGL).

Correct Response:

As you approach the minimum altitude you say, "Approaching minimum altitude, no clearance, going around", then you would do the go around procedure and setup for another landing. This shows the Instructor that you are prepared to make a decision and then act on it. In this case it is the correct and safe decision. The instructor has simply monitored your decision and actions. There was no need for QFI actions. You made a good captaincy decision. This is when you know as a QFI, that the student has 'got it'. In the debrief, the QFI would say something like:

Ok, so coming into land Bloggs, very good airmanship to recognize that we had no clearance and a good safe decision to go around. That is what I want to see. The go around was also flown nicely, well done Bloggs.

Incorrect Response:

a.   As you approach the minimum altitude you say, 'Normally here sir I would go around as we have no clearance, what would you like me to do? Sir, are you going to take control, we have no clearance?' This has all taken time and meanwhile confusion reigns in the cockpit and the aircraft descends below the minimum altitude and is reported by Air Traffic Control for getting too low without a clearance, potentially leading to a dangerous situation developing and the QFI having a report written against the aircraft.

b.   Do nothing and try to land on another aircraft requiring the QFI to take control to avoid a crash. This demonstrates fixation and loss of SA. This is both unsafe, and is a quick way off   pilot's course.

In both cases, the QFI would have taken control to prevent the situation from rapidly becoming unsafe. Whilst you may have had the correct information, you did not make a decision and act appropriately. The debrief for both a and b would be very similar:

Bloggs, you had no clearance. I was required to take control to prevent an unsafe situation from developing. You need to show me that you can understand the ATC directions and that you can make safe decisions without my help before I will let you fly solo. Today was not one of those days. If you see something that you are not happy about, then take action. Your performance will need to improve.

Here is an instructional video of actual cockpit footage of airborne instructional techniques utilized in the PC-9 Military turbo prop trainer thanks to our friends at AvgeekJoe: **Military Airborne instructional Technique** (https://www.youtube.com/watch?v=RWztGEqqKNQ)

CHAPTER 9
Putting It All Together

The following information is a summary of years of airborne instructional experience as tried and tested by the authors and countless students over the years. This has been condensed into just a few pages just for you. Please read it carefully and you will be on your way.

+ **First you must understand the aim and objectives of the programmed event.** Extract exactly what it is you need to know from the curriculum/syllabus. If you still have questions about the aim or what you need to know after reading the syllabus, speak to your Instructor, the day before. Make sure you know exactly what is coming up.

+ **Go to the publications.** You will be issued copies or given access to all of the relevant manuals you will need at the start of your course. It will be up to you to review your publications to ensure that you have all the information you need to fly. Go to the SATG for the techniques and details of the manoeuvre or procedure. Either write or draw (whatever works for you) the main points into your Slam book. Extract any limits or handling notes from the AFM or operating procedures/manuals (Standing Instructions, etc) and ensure this information is written down and learnt.

+ **Visualise the sequence (Chair Fly).** Go from start to finish including all the appropriate control inputs, where your eyes need to be looking, what to say on the radio, etc. Visualise again, this time introducing errors that must be corrected or problems to overcome – chair fly the mission.

✈ **Go to the pre-flight brief fully prepared.** It goes without saying but listen to the QFI. Ask appropriate questions if you have them. Don't be cocky, just be eager to learn. Remember you may think you know a lot, but you actually know very little about Military aviation, so be a good listener.

✈ **Fly the sortie.** Listen to your Instructor's advice on how to improve sequences whilst airborne. Practice being the captain and don't try to second-guess the Instructor. Sound positive and confident, without being arrogant or cocksure.

✈ **Listen in the debrief.** Take notes and provide your input. Be prepared for criticism. Use it as a tool. Make it work for you to make yourself a better pilot.

✈ **Close the loop.** Take away the lessons learnt on that sortie and incorporate them into your study for the next sortie to try and avoid making the same errors again. Re-visualise the sequence including your new knowledge.

BE PREPARED TO CHANGE

Military pilot's course will test your ability to think under pressure. You will most likely not be used to this. Your old boundaries will be stretched. Flying is far more than just an intellectual exercise – you must be able to deliver real time results, under daily public scrutiny, time and time again where the bottom line can be death. We don't say this to scare you but to reinforce that you will be taken out of your comfort zone numerous times in a potentially dangerous environment. But this is part of the thrill! Whilst a challenge, Military pilot's course is highly satisfying when well deserved success comes your way. So to meet those challenges, you must be prepared to change. The Military want decision makers, who just happen to be aircrew. Therefore, you must be prepared to make decisions. This will require some confidence, self-belief and knowledge. The Military don't want co-pilots. Don't stand on the edge of the course photo, don't hide or remain meek, be hesitant or shuffle about with your eyes down. **Hook in or fail.** Mice must learn to roar.

DEALING WITH STRESS

Stress can be placed on you or it can be self-induced. Place yourself for a moment in the cramped, hot cockpit with your engine running, radios crackling and clouds racing past and your friendly QFI listening. If you let it, stress can induce reluctance to make decisions, or conversely, a tendency to rush decisions. Stress also leads to a lack of awareness, one dimensional thinking, fixation and decreased memory recollection. It can lead to the 'Soda Straw' syndrome – if you let it. This is where you will be sweating the small stuff, fixating on the trivial and only seeing the limited picture as if you were looking at the world through a straw and missing out on most of what is going on around you. Imagine driving a car looking through a straw! Don't allow yourself to slide into this mentally constipated state. You can control it by being mentally tough and resilient. Recognize that you will make mistakes. Be ready to learn. Draw confidence from your solid foundation of preparation. Use controlled assertiveness to attack the problem. Doubt leads to hesitation - the enemy of confidence and effective decision making. The key is to ensure that you don't allow 'Sir' or 'Maam' to repress this controlled assertiveness. Remember the QFI wants to see a captain, someone ready and willing to accept a challenge, someone who believes in themselves, who wants to succeed, a positive student with 'tiger'. Be enthusiastic, smile, stand tall, be open and non defensive.

THE 'JOHN WAYNE'

Every course has one, but beware of the 'John Wayne' – no not the actor, but the cocky know-it-all. They are the course smart alec to coursemates and staff, who shoots from the hip (makes things up as he goes along) like his namesake, often with incorrect information and little prior thought. YOU WILL NOT LAST. Now John was a great

173

actor, but he would make a shocking pilot as you can see from some of his aviation movies! This is not only one of the quickest ways to fail but it is also dangerous. You don't want to be known as the perennial winner of the 'Cluster Cup' (an informal acknowledgement of a silly act), you want to be known as a mature, honest, hard working student pilot. Have a spring in your step, not a double holster and a swagger. Look good, feel good and sound good. Those last two words are very important – *sound good*. When flying, your voice is the window to your character. But don't overdo it!

As a QFI, I can tell straight away if a student is under / overconfident, decisive / indecisive just from their voice. Emanate positive vibes and be ready to accept and not shirk all challenges. After all, the Military wants you to pass! Remember at the end of the day, to pass a Military pilot's course, you will need to pass the following litmus test: The QFI needs to be sure that they would be happy to have their student captain an aircraft one day with a member of their family on board. Will you pass that test?

MOTIVATION

The key is your self-motivation. It is your rudder. It will give you direction provided it is targeted in the right areas. It also needs to be of moderate intensity – too little and you will allow yourself to become a 'mouse' and talk yourself out of passing, too much and you are 'holding on too tight' which will lead you to getting stressed and making mistakes. Perfection, whilst a noble aim, is rarely satisfied on a Military pilot's course. Your goals should be realistic. Set the bar at an appropriate level and keep it there. Talk to your Instructor if you need a motivation boost.

If you are struggling to remain motivated, seek help early, put your hand up. There are professional student counsellors who have seen it all before. It's worth fighting for, so seek help and remember, it's free! Loners often fall short. Remember - Military pilot's course is great, but what comes afterwards is even better! Keep keen and keep your chin up. The Military is trying to throw you the keys to your dreams, all you have to do is catch them.

AIR SICKNESS AND G

About ninety five percent of people will feel some degree of motion sickness at some time during their training, particularly early on in the course. This is completely normal. Even if you have not felt airsick on the basic trainer, the advanced trainer will test your stomach. This is because you now wear a helmet, an oxygen mask, have a g-suit inflate against your legs and your stomach as you are pulling up to 6 G with rolling manoeuvres. In most cases it is a matter of conditioning the body and shortly after commencing flying in either the basic or the advanced trainer, the sensation of motion sickness will pass. Persistent motion sickness can affect your concentration, co-ordination, motivation and information retention. The Military does have anti-motion sickness medication and, for worse cases, motion sickness eradication courses which are usually successful, for the very small percentage of aircrew who suffer from persistent airsickness.

The G force is equal to the force of gravity, which occurs in the vertical plane. Just like when you are thrown to the outside of a car when it turns a sharp corner, you are forced down into the seat when you turn sharply in an aircraft. Flying is in three dimensions (a car moves only in two dimensions) and this can be felt whilst turning sharply or during vertical manoeuvres such as a loop where an advanced trainer nominally pulls 4 G. This means that four times the force of gravity is acting on every part of you and your aircraft. Everything weighs four times as much. Your head for instance may weigh over 35 kg with a helmet on. Just lifting your arm can be virtually impossible at higher G. An advanced trainer can sustain above 4 G for some time, so you will be required to think and operate effectively in this environment. This is your new office! You will learn the Anti G Straining Manoeuvre (AGSM) but this will only partially offset high G manoeuvres and it is quickly fatiguing. However, you will get used to G quickly, but this is why we suggest you prepare with distractions and get and stay physically and mentally fit. Some elements of the pilot's course can be mentally and physically fatiguing and you need to be able to think clearly under these conditions.

HOW TO BOMB OUT

Here is a quick fire list of how to bomb out or be 'scrubbed' on a Military pilot's course. It doesn't mean that if you do one of these things it is all over, but just be mindful and avoid acting this way where you can. **Do not**:

- Fly to please sir (the Instructor). 'Is this ok sir?'
- Stay tense
- Fear failure (or success)
- Rush
- Avoid decisions
- Mumble and appear timid
- Keep your eyes down (in the cockpit and in dealing with people)
- Avoid QFI/CFI (Chief Flying Instructor)
- Be pessimistic or encourage negativity
- Be an oxygen thief, never contribute
- Just use rote learning. Robotic repetition of numbers without applying common sense
- Sweat minor details
- Ask stupid, helpless questions airborne
- Make excuses, tell lies
- Dwell on mistakes
- Drop your bundle unless it is perfect
- Pretend to know it all, you won't!
- Regard the whole exercise as a competition
- Be a loner and regard seeking help as 'weak ass'

SHARE YOUR EXPERIENCES

Don't try to single yourself out as the only person who knows what's going on, but rather by helping the group grow and learn together. Contribute positively. Don't become a 'One-er' (Only looks out for number 1, hoards information and thinks Military aviation is a competition). Your course mates will have some valuable tips, but you will only get them if you communicate effectively and are prepared to share your experiences. This is called 'Synergy' and will be of benefit to you. The Instructors are looking for leaders and officers who work well in a team. People who only look out for number one usually find the course a lot tougher than it needs to be. Remember, the Military is a team sport. The Military wants everyone to pass. Ideally, they would like all graduates to be able to fly fighters too (there is a constant shortage of fighter pilots). You are NOT competing with your course mates to get a particular job. There are enough jobs for everyone.

Share your lessons and listen to others, but don't believe all that you hear, especially when it comes from other students who think they know everything. There will be at least one on every course. These 'classroom QFI's' may exude a lot of confidence and knowledge but it is rarely correct, especially in relation to flying technique. Don't be one of them. Learn to filter out the 'duff gen' (false information).

I have flown with many students who, according to their course mates, exude confidence and nominate themselves to be the font of all aviation knowledge. They also tend to relay their own falsely inflated scores to their course mates to fit into the peer group. It is sometimes true that when I fly with people like this, they become timid children once airborne who won't make a decision and who, in reality, perform very poorly. They are portraying a false image. They are imposters and they will be found out. Don't get trapped into their vortex.

Don't try to be someone else. Just stay level headed. Be a good listener. Don't big note. Share your errors, but at the same time prepare hard and work hard. You will be seen as a reliable and genuine student whom your course buddies can easily relate to. It may help if you occasionally prep with other students as well. This could include students on the course ahead of you. Beware though as they may be 6 months ahead and tackling sequences that are not relevant to you now. Advanced students can provide useful information at times but they will often be busy with their own challenges as well.

ABOUT YOU

+ **You are always being watched!** This is not an attempt to make you paranoid but rather a word to the wise. It is not just your flying that the Military is interested in. It also wants to know what type of person you

177

are and get a feel for the strength of your character. They want to see what sort of person you are under pressure. So be aware of what you do after hours as well. You will be marked on your Officer Qualities (OQ's). Students who can fly well and would make a good pilot have failed the course due to unacceptable OQ's in the past. Remember they want an officer first, a leader.

→ **Be honest.** Always. The highest standards of integrity are expected. You will be trusted very quickly to take million dollar plus assets solo – don't blow your chance.

→ **Be keen.** A positive and helpful attitude goes a long way.

→ **Be proactive.** If something is wrong, let someone know early rather than letting it become a much larger problem later.

→ **Be yourself.** Its easier than trying to act…..

PEP TALK

Most people who walk through the door to commence Military pilot training want to, and should want to, fly fast jets. Sorry to offend any of our rotary wing friends, but this is a true fact and some of us are rotary wing! The cold reality is that, statistically, only about 60% of the course that started at BFTS will graduate with Wings. Of that, generally only the top 30 - 40% of candidates from each pilot's course will be given a preference to undertake fast jet training, and of those, only about 75% will end up graduating from their operational unit onto fast jet, some 18 months to 2 years later. These figures naturally vary from course to course and are in no means indicative of what may happen on your Military pilot's course. While the end result seems unattainable at first, the best thing you can do for yourself is to aim high, set realistic goals and stay focused on the near future, whilst keeping the end state as a distant, but achievable outcome. You must crawl before you can walk. Focus on the next day's events first, whilst having the overall vision of doing well and passing pilot's course. The rest will come in time.

Remember this analogy from previous chapters. When people climb hills or mountains, they don't just stare or focus at the top of the hill and become bogged down and depressed at the enormity of the task and therefore never take the first step. They are patient and well prepared for what's in store. They make a positive start, settle into a rhythm, one foot in front of the other begin to make incremental progress. They occasionally glance up, but that's about it. Surprisingly soon, your feet have carried you to the top. It's a gradual, slow process and the view is great! You will not be a pilot in a few weeks so there is no use running!

There is no doubt that a Military pilot's course will be the most exiting and rewarding training you have ever done, but inevitably there will be times when you will feel down. You may have failed a flight, or had a marginal ride (don't worry it has happened to the best of us). The workload may seem too high and getting higher by the day. You may have felt you did OK, but your Instructor has just spent 30 minutes pulling apart your performance. Remember that these things are all part of Military flying training, and can be expected by everyone at some stage. Even your Instructor was once in your shoes, possibly only a few years previously.

You will never stop learning throughout your course or in your Military flying career, and you must show self-discipline throughout to ensure that your preparation effort does not taper off. Coasting is dangerous and QFI are on the lookout for it. You will only get one chance at a Military pilot's course, so arrive at BFTS ready and raring to go for 12-15 months of hard work and great times. The course is a real challenge, but certainly achievable. At the end, you can feel justifiably proud to have earned your Wings. Always remember that the Military ultimately wants you to pass. The Defence Force always needs aircrew and it WANTS YOU to be one of them. It has selected YOU from a cast of thousands that applied because they BELIEVE you can do it. All you have to do now is prove it to YOURSELF.

It was near the end of BFTS, the 2nd last mission in fact. I thought it was a satisfactory flight, being the one before my BHT (Final BFTS Test). Unfortunately my QFI didn't think so and he pulled apart my handling of a basic emergency in the debrief. He said that whilst I handled the actual emergency actions well enough, I flew out of the area by 1.5 nm and that if this was the test, I would have failed it. He gave me a marginal score. I didn't even know that I had done it. Next thing you know, I had to sign a form acknowledging that if I failed my next sortie, the BHT, I might not get a second go and that could be it. Instead of dwelling on it, I chilled out firstly with a vigorous run. I tried to remain strong and I said to myself that this will not beat me. I reflew the sortie in my chair twice, applying appropriate suggested corrections, and prepped very hard for my test using my Slam book. I went in positive and confident. I had not failed any of my 50 flights to date and this wasn't going to be the first. I flew quite well. The QFI commented that I was well prepped and keen so he passed me.

CHAPTER **10**

A Pilot's Life

O btaining your Wings is your ticket to a great career as a Military pilot. You will now be eligible to undergo an operational conversion onto any aircraft within your service. Normally you will be notified before the end of pilot's course as to where your next posting will be and what aircraft type you will be flying. As mentioned, the final decision depends upon many factors, including your preferences and ability, but ultimately service conditions and vacancies at the time.

This chapter will give you brief outline of a typical Military career path after obtaining your Wings. It gives you a quick snapshot of life as a Military pilot. However, it cannot be too specific due to the great variation of flying jobs available within the Military organizations around the world as well as the fact that the flying and peripheral jobs within a squadron often vary daily themselves.

YOUR FIRST POSTING

Your first posting will be to an operational aircraft no matter what service. It is very rare to graduate as a newly qualified pilot and then be posted to a ground job. The practicalities of this are that whilst pilots will always be needed, some conversions onto aircraft can only be accomplished at a certain rate due to numerous factors. These include availability of aircraft perhaps due to serviceability or indeed actual Military operations, availability of instructional staff to accomplish the conversions and the numbers of personnel slotted to undergo these conversions. It basically boils down to timing. Whilst it is normal to undergo conversion training within a reasonably short time frame after graduating, conversion course start dates differ between aircraft types and services.

This may mean that whilst you will be posted to a Squadron, it may actually be a 6-12 month wait before your actual conversion starts in some extreme cases. During this time you may be required to conduct ground based duties whilst waiting. Many opportunities will come up including trips away where you can mingle with other aircrew and learn about the aircraft and its role. Sometimes slots come up earlier than anticipated on conversions for whatever reason and you may well be the first one notified to fill that position, sometimes at short notice.

Whilst delays do occur, your conversion should start reasonably quickly as the Military want you to apply the principles and skills you attained during your training to the specific operations, equipment and aircraft of your new squadron. So whenever you arrive at your conversion unit, do so with your notebook open and be ready to learn all over again. It's fun, you get to operate some fantastic hardware and do some pretty cool things, but like anything you will need to be prepared to work hard particularly in your first posting, because remember you and your newly graduated colleagues will be the most junior aircrew on the Squadron. In Australia, these junior aircrew are called 'Bograts'. You will start at the bottom.

TYPICAL CONVERSIONS

Here is a brief snapshot of some of the typical operational conversions and their rough duration that you could undertake after pilot's course. These vary significantly from nation to nation and are only a guideline. These timeframes are an indication of just a basic conversion to become qualified on type. Most of these aircraft require further training to become proficient in the role that they undertake. For example B737 AWACS conversion will allow you to fly the aircraft, but you will do further courses to become qualified on the capabilities that the aircraft has. Another example is that whilst you may learn to fly fast jet aircraft, you will be required to undertake various weapons courses to fully understand the capabilities and weapons limitations that may be at your disposal. Before you are cleared for operational roles such as going to war, you will need to do such courses and perhaps others.

Aircraft	Course Duration
BAe Hawk 127 Basic Jet Conversion	18 weeks
F18/ F16 Front Line Fighter	26 weeks
C130J Hercules	16 weeks
C17 Globemaster Heavy Transport	16 weeks
A330 Multi Role Tanker	18 weeks
B737 AWACS Airborne Early Warning	20 weeks
P3C Orion Maritime patrol	16 weeks
King Air 350 Light Transport	12 weeks
CL-604 Challenger Business Jet	6 weeks
AS350B Squirrel Rotary Wing	25 weeks
S70 B2 Seahawk Rotary Wing	12 weeks
Bell 206B Kiowa Rotary Wing	12 weeks
S70 A9 Black Hawk Rotary Wing	12 weeks

LIFE IN THE SQUADRONS

Although Military squadrons perform different roles commensurate with the aircraft that they fly, you can expect that your first tour will be a busy, but thoroughly enjoyable one. It will take time to become comfortable with the new aircraft type that you fly and this will only be achieved with consistent study, continually learning from more experienced Squadron members and exposure to the aircraft operating environment. You can expect that you will spend some time away from home. The duration of this time away will depend upon the aircraft type. Once you are cleared operationally you may be deployed to hostile locations for months or you may be posted to an aircraft carrier for instance. You can expect that you will fly with some very experienced captains, WSO, ACO, TACO, flight engineers and loadmasters. Soak up their experience. Be a human sponge. Listen well. You will learn quickly, have a great time and be exposed to some great flying, both in your home country and abroad.

When you are not flying, you will normally be involved in trip planning, mission preparation and odd squadron jobs. These 'odd jobs' will be your Secondary Duties and can include such things as base projects like Public Relations matters, amending flying publications, preparing briefs, missions and deployment planning, flying safety programs, recording squadron history, organizing squadron social events, etc. Be sure to perform these secondary duties well as mistakes and omissions here will highlight you as a poor performer on the ground, which reflects poorly on you as an officer.

Let's now take a closer look at the brief synopsis of life in your squadron as a Military pilot looking briefly at the various Military operational roles. As discussed, it can be very different from squadron to squadron as Military flying jobs don't lack variety.

FAST JET

One completion of wings, fighter and strike pilots will be required to convert to the lead-in fighter jet aircraft initially. Examples of this are BAe Hawk, T-38 and Aermacchi MB-339. After conversion, they will utilize this platform to undergo a form of Introductory Fighter Training (IFT). At course completion, these

baby fighter pilots will then convert onto a front line fighter jet such as the F-16 or F18 aircraft. It normally takes at least 6 months for an operational conversion and this will require a strong degree of application and determination to pass. Upon completion of this operational conversion course, new pilots will be posted to an operational squadron as a junior category D fighter pilot. You are now a junior 'knuck'. Now you will spend the next few years learning your 'trade'. Just about all of your sorties from now on will be solo, not in the 'tub' (dual trainer). You will now fly just about every day at least one or two sorties, slowly getting exposure and experience in the various roles and capabilities of the aircraft. You will conduct sorties involving ACM (Air Combat Manoeuvring) or 'dogfighting', BFM (Basic Fighter Manoeuvres), Air to Ground, Air to Air, Radar Intercepts, Bounce Missions, Combat Air Patrol and many of these will be in formation with other fighter jets. You will fly a lot of formation and at night and no doubt will be involved in major air exercises both in your country and abroad. Not all missions will be on a 100 mile 'bungee cord'; you will get to go places and you could be away from home a lot. So you will be busy.

Even after all the courses and ongoing learning you will have accomplished at your Squadron, you will be starting at the bottom. You will need to be humble and be receptive to advice provided by other squadron members who have more experience than you. When upgraded to C Category fighter pilot, you will then become fully operational and you will be cleared live into actual combat missions if required. Not only will you fly, but you will be flying sorties in the simulator, busy planning and debriefing missions, etc. So your day will be full, but it is ok as you will be living and breathing flying.

Although generic, the following is a brief snapshot of a possible day in the life of a fighter pilot in the Military:

0800 - 0830	Morning brief
0830 - 0915	Brief mission
0915 - 1000	Suit up/preflight/start
1000 - 1130	Fly sortie
1130 – 1145	Derobe/Post Flight
1145 - 1215	Review tape
1215 - 1330	** Debrief mission
1330 - 1430	Secondary Duties

185

1430 - 1730   Prepare for next days mission or fly another mission.

This profile is for a relatively short and simple mission. Some may take longer, especially involving multi ship formation missions or exercise scenarios. Also, most days you will fly two missions, so your day can easily be busier. Notice also that there is no lunch hour, sport or general faffing about. If the weather is suitable you can expect to be quite busy especially if you include your secondary duties.

** Typical debrief profiles look at salient safety points if any, that may have cropped up in the mission, points missing or incorrect from the pre-flight briefing, mission domestics, such as timings, radios, start, taxi, take off, taxi back, then the airborne mission is debriefed in detail and any learning points are extracted and enacted for the next sortie. This minimizes errors occurring two sorties in a row. These debriefs may involve the use of cockpot voice recorders, actual cockpit and head up display footage and radar derived data. It tells no lies!

At the end of your first tour, which is normally about 2 or 3 years, the normal options will be to either remain at your squadron for another tour, go on exchange and fly a fighter overseas or become a Qualified Flying Instructor or Fighter Combat Instructor. After that, you will probably return to an operational squadron to complete your ROSO. Junior fighter pilots don't often get ground jobs, but they do happen.

Check out these crazy French fighter pilots (they are obviously low to avoid radar!)
Crazy French Fighter Jocks[7]

---

[7] https://www.youtube.com/watch?v=7JeptX9yuDw

TRANSPORT / MARITIME

Transport or Maritime pilots will be undergo the required conversion training either at their posted Squadron or overseas. This will generally involve significant simulator training and some flying of the real aircraft. They will then become a category C or D copilot. This will enable them to occupy the right

hand seat and act as a copilot. You can expect to remain in the RHS depending upon the aircraft type for about 2 years before being considered for Captaincy. Your experience will grow commensurate with your exposure to the full capability and role of the aircraft. For example, some squadrons require further training to be able to conduct tactical operations such as flying under night visions goggles or operating the full suite of the Electronic capabilities of the aircraft. An example is the AEW&C (AWACS), which has quite a specific role in addition to learning to fly the aircraft. Another example is the operation of the aerial refueling aircraft such as the A330 MRTT or KC-135. Any additional training required for your aircraft type will normally be carried out at the Squadron.

A P3-C Orion or it's replacement the P-8 Poseidon is a maritime patrol aircraft. A maritime captaincy is a big deal. You will have a crew of a dozen or so operating modern electronic warfare in international, perhaps hostile airspace at perhaps 300 feet above the ocean at night dealing with highly classified information. It is not for dummies. Some of the crew members will have 15 years or more experience on the aircraft so as captain you need to earn their respect. This starts as soon as you step into the RHS as a copilot. But it is also very stimulating and satisfying work conducted in airspace all over the world. The international Military Maritime aircraft exercise 'Fincastle' for example has been held at various across the globe.

In the past, when pilots were posted to Maritime, they were rarely seen again as once maritime always maritime. They progress through co-pilot and on to maritime captain generally within about 3 years from conversion, subject to satisfactory performance. Once achieving enough captain experience, they may have a brief sabbatical as an Instructor before being sucked back into the 'Fish Head' world. Maritime pilots get a lot of flying and spend a lot of time away on deployment. It is a specialist role and as such they tend to remain in their area of expertise.

It is important that you work hard to ensure that you will be ready for command when your time comes. Command is not offered to everyone. You will need command time (captain hours) to be competitive for Instructor's course and to remain flying. The Military need captains, so work hard and become one.

There are always opportunities and vacancies that arise from time to time, but no matter which transport or maritime squadron you go to there will be more than enough exciting flying for you. After gaining some captain experience, transport pilots usually have the option of becoming a QFI, going to a ground job or remaining in the squadron as a senior supervisory captain. There are often overseas exchanges and Test Pilot positions available, but there are generally more pilots than positions available, so you will need to perform to be competitive. 'Trashies' will generally end up going back to their original aircraft type or another within Air Lift or Maritime Command after a spell.

VIP PILOT

A VIP pilot is not your typical 'trashie', so here is a brief snapshot of what to expect. The life of a VIP pilot usually involves a couple of days at work where the next trip is meticulously planned – flight plans, alternate airfields, fuel stops, parking, security, accommodation, catering, crew transport, timings, customs and quarantine, manifests and diplomatic clearances to name a few. Then you may fly the trip, which could be 1 -2 days or 2 -3 weeks depending upon the trip. There is no such thing as a 5 day week at VIP. Your mobile could ring anytime if you are on standby with only a few hours before you could be flying. You get to go to some great places though and you are flying very modern aircraft decked out with the latest cockpit software and luxurious internal fittings. This is a very different life to a fighter pilot for instance. 'Trashies' believe fast jet jocks fly all missions connected to a 200 km long bungee cord, which always makes them land back where they started from. In the transport world, you can expect to spend a significant time away from home.

I was posted to Canberra based 34 Squadron responsible for VIP movements direct from pilot's course. VIP Bizjets sounded like a cool posting. Well it got off to a flyer on arrival when I was told that I was required to attend aircraft conversion training for the next 6 weeks in a simulator in New York, USA! It wasn't all fun though; it was hard work learning to fly a modern bizjet from PC9's. The simulator was so capable that my first trip in the real aircraft, I was the co pilot flying the PM with 250 hours in my logbook.

ROTARY WING

The bulk of rotary wing flying is accomplished in the Navy, Army or Marines. Most initial rotary wing conversions begin on basic helicopters such as the Aerospatiale Squirrel or TH-67 and then onto their respective operational rotary wing type. There are many operational helicopters out

there – Seahawk, Blackhawk, Chinook, Tiger, Super Cobra or the formidable Apache. Again you are aiming to become a helicopter captain and in the Navy for instance, this will obviously involve a fair amount of time at sea.

Military rotary wing is some of the most exciting flying you can do. Helicopters by their very nature need to be 'flown' – there is very little use of autopilot or automation, so you will just about always have your hands and feet on the controls. Most of your flying is done close to the ground or water, so as such it can be very challenging and yet satisfying. Other than in the training role, Military rotary wing assets are often utilized away from home either on deployments, exercises or even in aid to the civilian community. You can expect to be involved in anything from troop lift, weapons delivery (firing rockets, machine guns or rotary cannons), counter terrorism operations, special forces operations, naval shipping support, anti-shipping and submarine warfare, ECM, surveillance and peace keeping operations. Also they provide aid to the civilian community in the form of medevac, disaster relief and resupply. As such there is no such thing as a typical day!

Army, Marine and Navy also have fixed wing pilots and they usually adopt a similar profile to Air Lift pilots as previously mentioned. On command, these pilots may have an additional option in that they can usually choose to remain fixed wing or undergo rotary wing conversions if vacancies exist.

I really enjoyed life as a Navy 'birdy'. I was posted to Sea Hawks and as part of their role; I operated from numerous ships and spent a lot of time at sea. This was a challenge in itself; try to land on a rolling deck perhaps at night with strong winds. It was a great life. You were at the sharp end of the ship with only a few other pilots on board. You had your own maintenance team and wherever the ship went, we went. We did plenty of flying and most of it was different. Anti-

sub one day, rappelling the next. It was a tight nit group and we worked well as a team to get the job done. I have a lot of respect for the Seahawk. It is a reliable and very capable aircraft.

TRAINING

Just like the day when you finish school, you don't normally walk in the next week as a teacher. It is normally the same in the Military. In order to become involved in delivering airborne instruction you normally need to be above average and hand picked as you need to be able to operate the aircraft proficiently and have the spare capacity to be able to 'quack' ie talk sense at the appropriate time and be able to fly an accurate demonstration. This will take some time to master. It's a bit like being able to drive a car safely whilst conducting a meaningful conversation on the mobile phone and to do both to a very high standard, but flying instruction is legal! This is why there are restrictions on driving whilst on a mobile phone as it reduces cognitive brainpower required to operate a car safely. So the Military will seek proven performance and command time before being considered for an instructional role, normally around 250 hours command on any Military type. You could be offered an instructional position commensurate with your experience base. This could be as a QFI, Fighter Combat Instructor (FCI or Top Gun) or QHI (Qualified Helicopter Instructor) or perhaps even a senior check captain. All require additional training. Fixed wing QFI training is done at a Central Flying School (CFS) like facility where pilots will attend Flying Instructor's course (FIC) which lasts for about 4 months. You will then normally instruct on the primary (single engine piston) - BFTS or basic (turbo prop) – AFTS for about 2 years and then be posted back to your aircraft type – Hornet, P3-C, etc. Then you can expect to conduct and instruct conversions onto your core aircraft type. Some QFI's remain in training and it can be very rewarding, ie posted to either BFTS/AFTS where you teach students to be pilots or to CFS where you teach qualified pilots to be instructors. It is from this CFS staff of QFI that some nations choose pilots to man their elite Aerobatic teams. These pilots are instructors of instructors and conduct Instrument ratings on qualified pilots who may already qualified to conduct instrument ratings on other pilots. These are called Senior Instrument Rating Examiner (SIRE) pilots.

Rotary wing QHIs are trained at the Military Rotary Wing Training School. Fast jet FCI's are trained at an Operational Conversion Unit (OCU) by other more experienced FCI's. This is a very demanding 6 month course and is quite role specific. So as you can see there is plenty of scope and variety outside your own squadron in the world of training.

TYPICAL CAREER PROFILE

As previously mentioned you can expect to serve for at least 10 years ROSO once achieving your Wings. You will normally be posted to a flying job after graduating and typically most flying tours last 2-3 years. So you can expect at least  2 more postings or tours during your ROSO. These postings may be an extension of your current tour or could be out of the squadron to a separate location such as FIC or perhaps a ground job. There are more pilots than cockpit positions available (more bums than seats) so it can be quite competitive to remain flying. Also every year more pilots enter the system, so you will find that as you become promoted and more senior, the flying opportunities diminish, despite gaining experience as a pilot and officer. The Military may need you to lead and supervise rather than conduct base level flying. Promotions will inevitably occur for executive positions such as Squadron Executive or Commanding Officers, Chief Flying Instructor, Flight Commander, higher level Wing staff and Command positions. This suits some people and not others, but it is a normal facet of life as a Military pilot and you should bear it in mind.

SOCIALLY

Along the way you will also form many strong friendships some of which you will have for life. Most pilots will tell you that their best friends are in the Military. This camaraderie that you build with people is often forged under operational cockpit crew conditions and this is a unique element of the Military. This leads to many social occasions that add spice to what is already an exciting lifestyle. Additionally, you will automatically be members of the Officer's Mess on your base or ship. The Mess is where there is an eating area, bar and recreational facilities. Each year there are often many functions held there such as balls, fancy dress gala occasions, etc and it can be a good way to socially unwind and make some good friends. You will miss this aspect of life once you leave the Military as it will never be the same.

FAMILY

Whilst the Military have made significant progress in this area, being a pilot means that you fly to places and often this means time away from home and family. Although it varies dramatically between aircraft types and service, on some aircraft types you can expect to be away from home for 6-7 months of the year on spasmodic occasions. Whilst great for single pilots, it can put stresses on the family at times. The Military do have an excellent support network, but the very nature of the job is that most of your job will be done away from home.

In addition, every 2 to 3 years you can expect to receive a posting. This could be to the same location, but it could also be elsewhere. So not only may you have to pack up everything every few years, but you may have to go through the inconvenience of a removal. Whilst you will normally be paid a disturbance and travel allowance and the removal is free, you will still be required to sort a new residence. Married quarters can be provided if entitled, but these removals can interfere with plans say to purchase your own home. If you have children, then you will have to enrol them in a new school and your spousal employment can also be a problem. The Military have a removals cell to assist with this transition and to make the process smoother.

TYPICAL MILITARY AIRCRAFT

Now, we will take a brief look at some typical military aircraft that you can expect to fly once you obtain your wings. Further specific details associated with the aircraft variant related to your Military can be found online.

Boeing Super Hornet

Bigger and even more potent than the 'Legacy' Hornet, the 2 seat F/A-18F Super Hornet will be a welcome addition to any Military. The aircraft will be fitted with the most advanced AESA radar available, a significantly upgraded electronic self-protection suite and some degree of stealth technology. It is also designed to have a great deal of cockpit commonality with the original Hornet making aircrew conversions a relatively straightforward process. Apart from being noticeably larger than the 'A/B' model Hornet, the Super Hornet is most easily recognised by the rectangular engine air intakes and the fact that it has 3 underwing pylons on each side (vice 2 on the F/A-18 A/B). It also has uprated 22 000 lb thrust GE F414 turbofan afterburnering engines.

Super Hornet demo: **Super Hornet**[8]

Joint Strike Fighter F-35 Lightning II

The JSF is being test flown now for potential introduction into operational service in the vey near future. The JSF is expected to be a true fifth generation, stealthy, multi-role fighter capable of superior air to air and air to ground weapons delivery.

---

[8] https://www.youtube.com/watch?v=X-1dbUZiu2Y

Hawk 127 Lead in Fighter

The Hawk is a tandem two seat jet, primarily used for initial fighter training to prepare aircrew for operational conversion onto a frontline fighter jet. The Hawk is not only an excellent fighter training platform, but it also provides a number of Military support roles as a light attack aircraft. With a cockpit based on that of a modern day  fighter, the Hawk has a HUD, 3 multifunction displays and a limited HOTAS system. External stores including extra fuel tanks, bombs, Sidewinder missiles and a gun can be fitted on the 7 external stations.

C-130J Hercules

 The Lockheed C-130 range of aircraft have been the backbone of Military transport for decades. The C-130J is the most comprehensive revamp of the Hercules aircraft to date. The C-130J provides international strategic air support, search and survivor assistance, aero medical evacuation and aid to the civilian communities. The J model is highly automated and contains state-of-the-art avionics. The flight deck features two head up displays (HUDs), four large multi function displays, five monochrome displays and Hands on Throttle and Stick (HOTAS). Integrated Navigation equipment provides the pilots with an automatic navigation solution from its Inertial Navigation System.

Boeing C-17 Globemaster

The C-17 Globemaster strategic airlift aircraft is a four-engine high-wing heavy transport with three times the carrying capacity of the C-130 Hercules (or the same load as 2.5 semi trailers). The capability allows the Military to rapidly deploy troops, combat vehicles, heavy equipment and helicopters anywhere in the world. It can operate out of airfields as short as 3,500 feet long - which is very impressive considering itsweight. The C-
17 is large enough to transport Chinook helicopters or the M1A1 Abrams tank. It has advanced avionics and can integrate seamlessly with NATO forces. It is a significant enhancement in terms of the ability to support national and international operations, and major disaster relief efforts.

AP-3C Orion Maritime Patrol

Maritime patrol is often performed by aircraft such as the AP-3C Orion. The AP-3C is responsible for a number of roles including Under Sea (anti submarine) and Surface (anti ship) Warfare, Maritime Surveillance, Naval Fleet Support and Search and Survivor Supply. Maritime Squadrons are charged with the duty of long range surveillance throughout a nation's borders. The 'P3' is also often called upon to perform it's specialized services on active duty overseas and carries torpedoes as well as the Harpoon anti shipping missile to deal with enemy vessels in times of conflict. Often on patrol at low level over the ocean and frequently at night, the mission outcome is determined by the strength and cohesiveness of the Military pilots on board. The Orion may work alone, or in conjunction with other aircraft or ships.

KC-30B A330 Multi-Role Tanker Transport (MRTT)

The MRTT is, in effect, a militarised air-to-air refuelling version of the Airbus A330. They serve already with various defence forces around the world. They are capable of refuelling fast jet, AWACS aircraft, JSF as well as transporting troops domestically or internationally. The aircraft will be normally fitted with both boom and probe type aerial refuelling systems. It will also be fitted with an electronic counter measures self-protection system, secure communications, Military data link and full glass cockpit. In its transport role, the MRTT is capable of carrying up to around 270 passengers and 34 tonnes of cargo.

Boeing 737-700 AEW&C (Airborne Early Warning and Control)

AWACS, as they are affectionately called, provide unprecedented airborne radar integration. It improves the capability and effectiveness of all other Defence Force flying assets, particularly when flying into potentially hostile areas. Normally fitted with an advanced high power MESA radar, a full complement of communication and datalink equipment as well as its own self protection suite, AWACS increase a nation's surveillance and air combat capability, provide air defence support for naval operations, and can assist in civil operations such as border protection and search and rescue. Communication systems including HF, VHF, UHF, Link-11, Link-16, UHF SATCOM and ICS may be fitted.

Boeing Business Jet (BBJ)

The 737 BBJ special purpose aircraft is used in various Defence Forces around the globe in a VIP and special purpose role. The BBJ combines the fuselage of the 737- 700 aircraft with a strengthened aft section, and the centre-section, wing and landing gear of the 737-800  aircraft. The BBJs are capable of being converted to a standard configuration of 36 passengers, or less. Normal crew consist of Captain, copilot and crew attendants. Extra pilots may be taken on longer overseas deployments.

Challenger CL-604

 The Challenger is a smaller VIP transport aircraft capable of carrying government officials, senior ranking members of the Defence Force and other VIP's both nationally and internationally. The Challenger features an advanced avionics suite, increased weight capacity and a greater fuel load than its predecessors such as the Falcon 900. The Challenger crew comprises 2 pilots and usually a single crew attendant.

ROTARY WING

S70 B2 Sea Hawk

The primary role of the Seahawk is to travel onboard Navy's FFG and FFH frigates and provide antisubmarine warfare and anti-surface surveillance. It extends the combat radius of the ship by finding, localizing and attacking, where appropriate, surface or submarine targets either independently or in

conjunction with other forces. A typical Seahawk mission involves up to four hours of low-level operations over the sea, by day or night, in all weather, often recovering to a ship's deck that pitches and rolls dramatically in heavy seas and usually wet with spray. Here is some Navy Rotary Wing action: **Navy Birdies**[9]

AS350B Squirrel

Now mainly used in a training role, the Squirrel light utility helicopter is quite popular with militaries around the world. Its training role includes the conversion of pilots to rotary wing flying, preparation of pilots for operational flying as well as observers and aircrewman for their basic utility training.

---

[9] https://www.youtube.com/watch?v=b-LAJIz8f6I

The MRH -90 Multirole Helicopter

The multirole Eurocopter MRH 90 is now enjoying operational service within various branches of the Military. This provides opportunities for joint fleet management, greater operational flexibility and efficiency through common operational, training and logistic systems and a capability to rotate personnel, aircraft, spare

parts and role-specific equipment between troop lift, special operations and maritime support commitments. This aircraft is sequentially replacing Blackhawk, Seahawk and SeaKing across the rotary wing spectrum.

CH-47D Chinook

The 'Chook' has operated for over 50 years now in one form or another. It continues to serve well as a heavy lift helicopter and is highly distinguishable with its twin rotors and absence of tail rotor. As the Chinook can self deploy with all it's own required support, it can readily conduct operations from forward operating bases or from a sailing ship. Fitted for Night Vision Goggles, it is invaluable for artillery, vehicle and heavy equipment movement in the field 24/7. Cargo can be loaded internally via a rear ramp or slung underneath the fuselage and connected with cargo hooks. The aircraft now serves for more than 15 countries worldwide in numerous variants.

Eurocopter Tiger Attack Helicopter

Built with the latest systems integration concepts and materials technology, the Armed Reconnaissance Helicopter is a huge step forward in capability for an Military. Advanced avionics including a helmet mounted sight, comprehensive self protection system, laser tracker and Hellfire missiles ensure the combat edge against ground targets. The tandem crew of two has the pilot normally sitting in the front seat and the gunner/mission commander in the rear seat. The largely carbon fibre/ kevlar fuselage has excellent strength and resistance to small arms fire. The Tiger will prove a tremendous and personal experiences from numerous sources in all three Services about recruiting, training and life as an force multiplier to troops on the ground as it provides intelligence and reconnaissance to enable ground commanders to make effective real time decisions. Not only that, but it can pack a punch when required.

Here is some rotary wing action....cool eh!
Military Rotary Wing action[10]

FURTHER OPPORTUNITES

The flying opportunities within the Military are improving and changing all the time. This is one of the bonuses of life as a Military pilot. Indeed since we wrote out first Military aviation book in 2004, most Military's will have upgraded and even replaced many elements of their aviation assets including

---

[10] https://www.youtube.com/watch?v=Cdh4PMg1nmo

many of the aircraft themselves. No doubt there will be an exciting array of new aircraft and all of them need pilots.

As you progress in your career, there are also many other courses and areas of further training that will interest you. The Military wants to make sure you are always learning and improving. Numerous courses such as Military Weapons, Introduction to Joint Warfare, Flying Safety Officer, Qualified Flying Instructor, Fighter Combat Instructor, Test pilots and many others may be available depending on your experience at the time. There is also extensive ongoing training covering such aspects as Crew Resource Management, Aviation Risk Management, Human Factors, Leadership and Communication to name but a few. On top of this, there are also opportunities to travel and fly other nation's aircraft on international exchange postings. As a Military pilot, there is always something new around the corner. The sky literally is the limit and you get paid to be there!

CHAPTER 11
Post Military
Your Options

You may be wondering why you are reading a chapter that deals with the end of your Military career before you have even started. Well, you will have to leave at some time whether you had a short or a long career. Believe us when we say that the time just 'flies' and that sooner than you think, you will have had a rewarding career in the Military, flown some of the best aircraft around the world, experienced exciting situations, and made life long friendships. So what happens when the time comes for you to ponder leaving the Military for the big wide world out there? What opportunities await you? What skills do you have that can be put to good use in the civilian world?

DEPARTURE

Prior to your leaving, most Military organizations will need you to return all public issued flying clothing such flying suits, boots, aircrew watch, aircrew leather jacket, field equipment, etc. You are normally permitted to keep your Military dress uniforms and some flying clothing such as flying socks and gloves.

Prior to you separating from the Military, members can normally expect to undertake a form of resettlement training, which of course is free of charge. It is highly desirable especially if you have gone straight from school to the Military and have never worked in the 'real world'. The course will contains topics such as:

✈ Education and career transition assistance schemes
✈ Transition administration to civilian life
✈ Civil accreditation
✈ Financial planning and investments
✈ Government entitlements (Entitled allowances, pension asset test, Health care cards, claims processing)
✈ Legal consideration (Wills, Estate planning, trust funds, family law)
✈ Franchising/small businesses advice
✈ Real estate education
✈ Insurance requirements for civilians – medical, life insurance, etc
✈ Compensation and advocacy
✈ Service in the reserves
✈ Employment in Government or Public Service advice
✈ Superannuation/Pensions (Advice here can save you thousands!)
✈ Recruiting agencies, job opportunities
✈ Preparing for small business
✈ How to market yourself and CV preparation

The separation process can seem daunting, especially if you are about to embark on a new and unfamiliar career path. You may for instance have tracked direct to the Military from school and have never had a civilian job. Most of the resettlement process is merely to ensure that all the administration has been done prior to you leaving the Military. Your decision to leave the Military is not viewed as though you are deserting the team, or leaving the organization in the lurch, but as an action you have undertaken following at least 10 years of service, and in general there is no acrimony. Clearly the Military will always be reticent to see highly specialized staff such as aircrew leave, however there is no overt pressure preventing your departure, assuming all Return of Service Obligations have been met. Don't forget, the Military are not silly. They plan for the number of pilots they will need utilizing historical pilot attrition rates based over a long period. Effectively, they plan on many departures around the ROSO commitment, so there is no ill feeling at all.

In many cases the Military will take you back if that opportunity arises. Some times your 'greener pastures on the outside' don't work out for some reason. This is actually relatively common. You may have a family or health issue that necessitates that you take a break from the Military, such as leave without pay. In this case of if you actually formally resign, never burn your bridges as you never know, you may want to have your old job back. You won't realize how impressive the skills that you have obtained in the Military are until your reach the civilian sector. You are very well trained and highly regarded in many skillsets. As such many civilian employers find a Military pilot a very good employment prospect. You will be have a high level of self-discipline, be punctual and you will be trustworthy. You are a known and trusted quantity based on the strong and long standing tradition of those who have left before you.

The flip side is that many Military organizations would most probably be keen to take you back especially if you have maintained your core skills or better still, gained even more experience. A good example of this is a Military pilot who has become an airline pilot who now may be Airbus rated. This would be attractive to the Military particularly if they are about to acquire Airbus aircraft. Initiating a pool of experienced pilots from scratch is an expensive and time-consuming process. Having ex-Military pilots with significant Airbus experience gained from another employer working either part time or full time is a win-win for everyone. Another example is a Qualified Flying Instructor who may have the left the Military and continued instructing on other Military aircraft overseas. The Military would generally welcome these experienced aircrews back if they reapplied, if positions were available, particularly if they had significant experience on an aircraft type just acquired by your nation's Military. You may not be immediately employed direct into a flying position, but you may not have to wait long. Again you would be value adding to the Military experience base and they would be employing a 'known product'.

I left the ADF after 15 years and took up civilian flying. After a few years I found it a tad boring when I noted an advertisement in the Australian newspaper stating that experienced Military pilots are encouraged to reapply if they so desire. When I contacted them I was offered Flying Instructor's course and I did another 5 years full time before moving to the Reserves.

EDUCATE YOURSELF

Often whilst in the Military and flying with a Squadron, the hardest thing to do is find time to learn about a new vocation. Remember to try to make time. You will be investing in your own future career in much the same way you are currently investing in your Military career. A few simple tips to get you thinking are as follows:

- ✈ Explore your interests
- ✈ Investigate University/College courses that interest you
- ✈ Speak to colleagues
- ✈ Speak to careers advisors/ employment agencies
- ✈ Research and prepare for your next vocation (be discreet, don't bring your Cathay Pacific notes to work!)
- ✈ Set yourself goals and timeframes in which to achieve them
- ✈ Aim high

The most important point here is not to leave thinking about what you would like to do after the Military until you are ready to resign. This is last minute thinking and usually leads having to make a rushed decision at a major career crossroad. There is no doubt that within the Military there are opportunities for brilliant careers, but most people will not stay forever and often leave shortly after their ROSO expires. Be ready for it in case you are one of them!

RESERVES

Joining the Military Reserves program in your respective service can be an effective method of easing out of the service. You can have some say in your final location as there are often many reserve units scattered throughout the nation, but it will depend upon what job in the Reserves that you end up doing. There is normally a minimum monthly commitment in the active reserves for each service. The Military gains a trained specialist (albeit part time) and you get to earn some extra cash and enjoy the benefits of the service without potentially being required to undergo removals. In some cases the Military may even pay your employer whilst you are undertaking reserve duties. Everyone wins.

When you resign from the service, you will normally need to give notice of 3 months of effective service. This is so that the Military can prepare for your exit by finding and posting a replacement etc. You have two options when you do resign. You can resign completely (sever all ties with the Military) or you can join the reserves. All Military services have an active or inactive reserve scheme. This means that you can enrol in the active or inactive reserve on exit from the Service.

Active Reserve: The active reserve means that you leave the full time service and can now work for the service in a part time role or on a contractual basis. You will be able to work up to about 130 days per year but this can vary greatly between services. It is attractive  as you may have an commercial helicopter job for instance which may allow you some time to be able to offer your services to the Military on a part time basis. You may wish to remain current on your primary aircraft type or be available to instruct in the simulator for instance. This adds to the experience base of the Military and you will get paid in some cases tax free dollars whilst working as a reservist. As mentioned, there may be some scope for the Military to compensate your company for your time away from your normal day job subject to stringent conditions. So it can be an attractive option for some and is definitely worth thinking about. It also makes re-entry full time back into the Military a much smoother process than resigning completely if you change your mind later, which is surprisingly common.

Inactive Reserve: This is where you leave the service full time, where all you are required to do is keep the Military updated on your current details. No work is required. It is a paperwork exercise only. This can be a good option as your name remains on the books for normally 5 years or so and again it makes it a whole lot easier to get back into the Military should you so desire. It is also easy to contact you in times of a National Emergency. You can also enroll to be sent Defence updates via email including Defence news blogs, periodicals, events, etc.

WORLD AT YOUR FEET

Now that you have spent a good deal of time in the Military (at least 10 years), it is fair to say that some degree of 'Institutionalisation' is inevitably ingrained. You will be intimately in tune with the Military lifestyle, and for many, it is a comfortable and rewarding life. For others, the urge to move into the private sector is also an exciting proposition. Military pilots do not just leave for the airlines or contract work (although many do) and are capable of many more working roles than flying aircraft. If you have been through the Academy and obtained a tertiary qualification, you will be well positioned to compete for the myriad of jobs existing outside. Many pilots, whilst still serving in the Military, undertake part time studies in the Arts and Business fields, obtaining Marketing and Business degrees with the intention of entering aviation related Management positions. Others take up overseas positions. Here is an example of just one successful business:
http://www.afterburnerseminars.com

Indeed, a number of colleagues who have exited the Military have taken up medical studies and are now practicing doctors. Others have entered politics, become lawyers, become company directors or started businesses. Some just retire. Like exiting any job, the options are limited only by your imagination.

THE AIRLINES

The simple truth is that the major airlines like Military pilots. Why? The Military produces a known quantity that airlines can relate to and rely on. The training we have received has been professional and consistent. This is not to say that other institutions and schools do not produce outstanding pilots, but that the Military is a renowned worldwide institution with a long heritage when it comes to training, developing and maintaining pilot and leadership skills. However, we are not suggesting that all Military pilots are suited to, or gain entry to commercial airlines. There is no right of passage, and recruiting standards are very high and positions as aircrew on airlines are traditionally very competitive. However, with a history of disciplined study habits, thorough training, a professional work ethic and consistent ongoing quality assurance testing, you are well positioned to potentially embark on an airline career if you choose.

Should you be successful in joining an airline, it will more than likely be as a second officer. This can be quite a different role than you are accustomed to. You may have been a captain of a Boeing 737, a fast jet pilot, or a flying instructor, and now you are relegated to a non flying position in crew of three. The worst thing that you can do is to act as though such a position is beneath you given your flying career to date. You will not really be joining for the flying, as it is just about all autopilot. You will be joining for the lifestyle. You have been trained in the Military to fulfill a role in the profession of arms, and this is very different from the commercial aviation role, which is dominated by the dollar. Speaking of dollars, your first airline job will normally mean that you will take a pay cut to leave the Military and you may even have to pay for your airline endorsement which could be over $30 000 USD. There are exceptions and of course you have to weigh up remuneration versus lifestyle, stability, location, etc when you make your final decision.

As with all things, approach airline flying with an open mind if it is your chosen profession post Military. Be ready to learn new skills and be ready to drop any prejudices. You will start as a minnow in a large ocean. But believe in your training, your pedigree. You will be well placed, but be humble, progress steadily and the civilian aviation world is your oyster.

GOOD LUCK...

Whatever you have chosen to do following active service in the Military, you will take with you years of experiences and memories, and continue to build upon the values and skills imbued upon you from the moment you first walked into your Initial Officer Training, so long ago. You will miss the Military, there is no doubt about it. But some day you have to move on. Good luck!

CHAPTER **12**

Frequently Asked Questions

The following chapter details some typical FAQ in relation to employment within the Defence Force as a Military pilot. We have tried to keep the questions general in nature due to the natural variation of conditions of service within the global Military community. This chapter divides the FAQ into sections to help you find what information you are looking for more efficiently. Be sure to check out your Military's website for the finer details.

PAY AND ALLOWANCES

Q. Do I have to pay for meals and accommodation whilst undergoing training or living on the base?

A. Single members under training will normally be required to reside in accommodation provided on the relevant training base. They will also have three meals cooked daily in the Student's/Cadet's Mess. Students will be required to contribute an amount of their pay towards these rations and quarters (R & Q), which is well below market rates. It is usually less than 10% of salary. Members with Dependants (MWD) who have been categorised Members with Dependants Separated (MWD(S)), will normally be accommodated on base or in off base dedicated married quarters or obtain rental assistance to live in a non Military house or apartment. In either case, the overall package will ensure that you will pay only around 50% of market rent.

They are not required to pay for meals or utilities, as they are usually paying rent and other living expenses for the rest of their family at another location.

Q. Do I pay tax?

A. Full-time Defence personnel are required to pay income tax the same as any other employed person within their home country. Some countries do not charge tax and therefore a salary would be tax free. There may be an option to package your salary under a salary sacrifice arrangement which allows you to spend before tax dollars on certain approved expenses. The Military also has well established pension schemes where the Military will contribute towards your pension during your time in service. Part-time personnel (Reservists) do not normally pay income tax on their Defence wage.

POSTINGS

Q. Do you get a choice where you are posted? (Location of employment)

A. At any time, you are given the opportunity to express a preference for the localities and also the specific jobs to which you would like to be posted. There are many names for these such as Personal Preference Plan (PPP). While Defence will try to fulfil your posting preferences, your ultimate posting location will depend upon a combination of Service requirements and vacancies at the time, your performance in your current Military position, your aptitude and attitude towards your job and the personnel around you. This will most probably be away from your initial recruiting entry location. Try to become familiar with the existing operational squadrons and where they are situated, as they are normally where you will be going! The Military will cover all costs associated with removals.

Q. How often are you posted to a new location?

A. Once Military pilot's course has been completed, you will be posted to an operational flying unit for further training onto your applicable aircraft type. Generally, a posting is for 2 to 4 years. However, a posting may be shorter or longer due to Service requirements. After 2-4 years you could be posted back into the same unit for a further tour of duty (which means that you don't actually move at all) or you could be posted to another location and/ or aircraft type or even a ground job. This is just a normal part of the Defence Force life and adds variety to your employment options.

Q. What happens to my spouse and children if I join?

A. Throughout initial training until completion of wings, your spouse and children (if applicable) will be provided with Military subsized housing where your rental costs will be subsidised. Normally this means that your spouse and children will accompany you to your relevant training location. Removals will be conducted and paid for by the Military. On completion of your Military pilots's course your spouse and children will be provided with a removal at Military expense to your new posting locality. The particulars of each removal are determined in consultation with the serving member taking into account their wishes. The Defence Housing Authority or the like administers housing for Defence Force members. They will usually have a large number of properties on their books in your gaining locality, but your timing into the area will determine what is available when you arrive. The accommodation standard is generally good and you can expect to pay about 50% of the market rent which is another side bonus of the Defence Force remuneration package.

WORKING HOURS

Q. Do I get weekends and public holidays off, and can I go home on weekends?

A. Except during Initial Officer Training where leave will most likely be restricted, Military pilots under training will generally only be required for duty from 0730-1700 Monday to Friday. The rest of the time is for personal leisure or study as required. However, from time to time, Military members are required to work additional hours during weekdays, weekends, and public holidays subject to Service requirements. This is particularly the case in operational squadrons where the very nature of Military aviation requires that working hours are anything but regular and routine. For instance many squadrons will deploy on exercise or operations for weeks or even months.

During this time you will get some time off but usually only at the exercise location. In this case you may not see your family for many months and you may work some 7 day weeks.

You will generally not be given time off in lieu or paid overtime for this. You will be paid a service allowance or form of it, which is a permanent component of your salary and it compensates you for short notice deployments, weekend and overtime work done due Military requirements.

ACCOMMODATION / FOOD

Q. What is the standard of accommodation and food like?

A. Generally, the standard of accommodation on Defence bases is quite reasonable and is being upgraded regularly. During initial training new members will be provided with single room, air conditioned (usually) accommodation with communal facilities such as bathroom, kitchenette and living room. Food is prepared by trained cooks and is generally of a high standard with many choices available. These include vegetarian and low fat options for instance. This area of the Military is improving all the time.

Q. Do you have to live on base?

A. Single people are encouraged to live on base during training. Married or de-facto people will be eligible for Defence Housing and are not required to live on base during training if their spouse is in location with them. Once initial officer training and pilot's course is completed, single people are not required to live on base.

Q. Can I get housing assistance?

A. If you have legal dependents (e.g. spouse, children) then you will be offered Defence housing
assistance at your posting locality. If you are single, Defence may offer rental assistance payments at your posting locality.

FACILITIES

Q. What facilities are available on base, and what are these facilities like?

A. The facilities available vary from base to base. Generally, each base has accommodation facilities,
sporting facilities (e.g. gym, pool, playing fields, tennis courts), leisure facilities (e.g. bar and recreational clubs, sporting clubs), tailor, hairdresser, pharmacy and some shopping facilities (e.g. Px, canteen, hairdresser). Generally, these facilities are maintained to a high standard, and cater for a diverse range of interests (e.g. various hobby and sporting clubs). There is also a welfare store that may allow you to sign out things like Scuba gear, kayaks, camping gear, surfboards or other recreational equipment for a nominal fee.

PHYSICAL FITNESS

Q. Do I always have to do physical training?

A. There will be Physical Training (PT) requirement on all training courses. After course completion, physical training and the condition of your body is up to you, although most Military organizations do have regular PT sessions built into most days. You can do as much or as little as you like, however, to ensure an operational capability, Defence requires its personnel to maintain a good level of physical fitness and all members of the Military are required to pass fitness tests to a minimum base fitness level regardless of their employment.

Q. As a pilot, will the Military be happy with me boxing or base jumping?

A. Not really. The Military is not a fan of dangerous or high risk sports. Depending on the activity, however, permission can be sought via your CO but will probably include some restrictions.

FURTHER TRAINING/EDUCATION

Q. Are there any opportunities to further my study?

A. Yes. The Defence Force encourages its members to further their education by providing financial and leave support. However, you will most probably be too busy in your first two or three years in the Military to contemplate further schooling. Education Officers (EDO) are usually good sources of information on this topic. Most bases will have at least one EDO.

RETIREMENT

Q. When do you have to retire?

A. Maximum retirement age as Military aircrew in the Defence Force normally ranges between 55 to 60. Having said that, there are not many Military aircrew around who are over 50 still flying full time. As you get older and go up the rank structure, there are less flying positions available for you to fill as they seek your Military experience now to be directed more towards command and leadership positions.

Q. Can you still called up after the leaving the Military?

A. All personnel who join the Defence Force usually become members of the 'Inactive'
Reserve for five years after leaving permanent service in the Navy, Army, Marines or Air Force. This is, in effect, an administrative exercise only and other than providing the Military with your latest address, requires no other commitments. It allows the Military to maintain a database of recently trained personnel to boost numbers in case of national emergency. You would not be eligible to be called up if you were forced to leave the Military for some reason or is you disqualified yourself from one of the minimum criteria for entry. You may choose to sever all ties completely on discharge, which is fine as well.

TRANSFERS

Q. Can I transfer to another country's Military?

A. The opportunity to request for transfer from your current Military to another Defence Force does exist, but applicants must satisfy normal immigration requirements and have the appropriate qualifications and skills levels. Obviously there must be an arrangement in place whereby the two Defence Forces have an alliance! Normally the relevant Embassy staff in your country can help and they will put you in touch with a Military Attaché for further advice.

Q. If I take this job can I change over to another job/service at a later stage?

A. Although the opportunity to transfer between jobs and/or Service does exist, it is not guaranteed. The option is only available subject to Service requirements. It depends on the staffing levels in the job that you are currently in and the staffing levels in the job to which you wish to transfer. Remember, you cost a lot to train, so they don't want to lose you early to become infantry for instance. Each Service generally (but not always) requires a person to serve their entire ROSO commitment post wings, before they will be considered for transfer. This provides some economic return of service for the training provided. There are often also opportunities to spend time flying for another service whilst still in your original service (on loan).

LEAVE

Q. How much leave do I get per year?

A. All Defence personnel are normally granted 20 days recreational leave annually. Aircrew, normally receive an additional 10 days leave taking the total to 30 days (work days only are counted). Normally it is a requirement that you exhaust this leave every year. Time on deployment can increase this leave entitlement once the deployment has ceased. Also during your service, you will accrue a long service leave entitlement.

Q Can I get leave if one of the members of my family get sick or dies?

A. If you are a single member then you will normally be able to take compassionate leave to visit a sick or dying relative and sometimes the Military will pay for your trip if it is to next of kin. If you are married then again the Military will do their best to accommodate your request. The Military will try to accommodate your request even if you are deployed on overseas operations (subject to operational restrictions and depending upon the nature of the emergency). Most Military's are very good at this compassionate aspect of service life and Commanding Officers will normally exercise the full power of their discretion on such matters. The Military also need to be on the lookout for abuse of the system as some may use this as a tool to avoid active operations.

DE-FACTO RELATIONSHIPS

Q. Does the Military recognise de-facto relationships?

A. Yes. Applications for de-facto relationships are to be forwarded to the Commanding Officer at the unit you are at for further consideration and approval. A person in a recognised de-facto relationship is normally treated as a married member for entitlement purposes.

JOINING/ENTRY REQUIREMENTS

Q. I'm 17 years old. Can I join the Defence Force?

A. Yes. The Military normally observes a minimum voluntary recruitment age of 17 years, which does vary between the services. The recruitment of all minors must be voluntary, and all minors must have the written consent of a parent or guardian. As evidence of proof of age, all persons wishing to join the

Military must present an original or certified copy of their full birth certificate to their recruiting officer. Gone are the World War I days of joining at 14!

Q. Does one have to be a Citizen?

A. Applicants must be a citizen of the nation whose Defence Force they want to join or have permanent residency status and be willing and eligible to become a citizen. Proof of application to become a citizen is required and if the application is rejected, service will be terminated.

Q. How do I stand if I have committed an offence years ago?

A. All applicants will undergo a mandated background and criminal history police check. Defence does take into consideration the nature of the criminal history of an applicant when assessing his/her suitability; this is done on a case by case basis.

THE RECRUITING PROCESS

Q. What is the process for applying?

A. See Chapter 1 and 2 for more information regarding the entry process and how to prepare for it.

Q. How long does it take from submitting my application until I will be required to attend application day?

A. Generally, all applicants will attend an application day within 2 months of the application being received. However, this may vary depending on the number and type of applications being processed by Defence, at the time.

Q. What happens if I don't like the Defence Force after I join, is there a cooling off period?

A. Generally speaking ROSO is only valid once Wings are obtained. However, this is not always the case, so check first. A self induced resignation is available though not encouraged prior to this point. Even someone who gets 75% of the way through a Military pilot's course has cost the Military more than $1M, so the Military will encourage you as an officer to take up other Defence Force options of employment (eg. Supply, Air Traffic Control, etc). During officer training, personnel can resign at any stage by giving 3 months notice provided they do not have a return of service obligation for other types of training. At a Defence Force Academy once you have completed 2 years of study you will normally have a ROSO. Prior to 2 years, generally speaking, you can resign with 3 months notice.

Q. What subjects should I study at school?

A. Certainly English and Maths (Not a basic version) and at least one science subject (Physics tends to have the most relevance). Getting a broad education will do you a great deal of good, whether you get in or not. Checkout your local Defence Force website for the latest minimum educational requirements.

MEDICAL

Q. What medical restrictions govern my eligibility to join?

A. Entrants will be required to carry out not only their primary flying duties but will also be expected to perform arduous duties of a general service nature both in peace and war, under field conditions, in extremes of climate and without more than basic medical or dental support. Applicants must therefore be free of any illness or disability that would prevent them from carrying out these duties throughout their Service life. You will be given a rather detailed and probing medical questionnaire to take home and complete. For more information, consult Chapter 1.

Q. What is the Military's policy on Marijuana smoking? Can I use it in my off duty hours?

A. In general, no. Most Defence Forces has a zero tolerance to self-administered illegal drugs. The use of marijuana for instance is not allowed and random drug and alcohol testing is conducted to ensure compliance.

Q. What is the minimum height for joining the Military?

A. Generally the minimum height for joining the Military is close to 152 cm without shoes. Pilots may have further restrictions than some other 'backenders' due to cockpit restrictions particularly in ejection seat aircraft. There will also be a minimum weight due to ejection seat limits which mostly impacts females.

FLYING TRAINING

Q. Does civilian flying help to pass pilot's course?

A. Not really. There are many successful Military aircrew who had never flown an aircraft before joining. It may help in the very earliest stages of BFTS but that is about it. Civilian pilots generally do not get exposed to the same type of flying that the Military does. It can also be detrimental by teaching bad habit patterns that must be dispensed with on a Military pilot's course.

Q. What will happen to me if I don't pass Military pilot's course?

A. That would depend on many factors including; did you go to a Military academy or not, have you a demonstrated interest in another job in the Military, how far did you get on Military pilot's course and your officer qualities. There are primarily 2 options: Stay with the Defence Force in some other role or get out altogether.

Q. Can I do work experience with the Military prior to joining?

A. Yes, depending on your location and available units. However, it is necessary for you to write to the local Defence establishment directly. Defence Force recruiting does not normally organize the work experience program.

FLYING CAREER

Q. Can I change aircraft types throughout my career?

A. Yes. Not only can you, but you will be expected to at some point, even if it is only to leave your
operational type to become an Instructor at one of the training schools. If you want to fly another type, go through your chain of command (your supervisor and CO) and request it through normal Military channels.

Q. How many years flying can I expect?

A. On average, most would fly for about 8 years out of 10. Some may fly for 20 years straight before
getting a ground job but that is unusual. It often happens that aircrew particularly pilots may get a 2 year ground job after 4-5 years operational flying as there are more pilots than flying positions. From there, most would return to flying duties.

Q. What is a Ground Job?

A. A job or posting where the primary function is not physically flying aircraft, but may be flying related. There are many different ground jobs that require aircrew to fill the billet due to their specialist knowledge. They are generally not more than 2 or 3 years in length and can be as rewarding and challenging as flying. There are too many ground jobs in the Military to list but a couple of examples may be anything from Wing Flying Safety Officer or Range Safety Officer to Assistant to the General staff. Some may even involve some limited flying either in Military aircraft or civilian aircraft.

Q. Are there any concessions made for female aircrew in the Military?

A. Female aircrew are treated just like males both during training and post graduation. There is a strict EEO (Equity and Equal Opportunity) policy in the Military to ensure a pleasant working environment for all members.

"Thanks for reading and good luck with your aspirations"
Mal Bloggs

If you like our book then please rate it. If you have any feedback or suggestion from improvement please email us directly at *bhorizonenterprises@yahoo.com.au*

We do rely on our loyal readers, the new recruits to tell us if we have got this right. We are continually striving to supply you with the best Ebook possible that is accurate, updated and spot on when it comes to help you become a Military aviator.

Published by **Blue Horizon Enterprises Pty Ltd**

Proud authors of:

Book 1   **"How to be a RAAF Pilot"** April 2004 (Print and pdf format).

Book 2   **"WINGS: How to become a Pilot in the RAAF"** Edition 2.0" first published November 2005 (Print and pdf format).

Book 3   **"WINGS: How to become a Pilot in the ADF"** Edition 3.0" first published January 2010 (E-book pdf format).

BLUE HORIZON ENTERPRISES Pty Ltd
WINGS - HOW TO BECOME A MILITARY PILOT
First Edition
ISBN 978-1-925128-82-6

Everything you need to know about how to become a Military pilot. Completely revised and updated, **Wings – How to become a Military Pilot** Edition 1.0 is filled with information, personal experiences and practical advice on:

- ✈ Specific pilot entry requirements for the Defence Force
- ✈ The current recruiting process
- ✈ Insight into the training system of the Defence Force

✈ Guidance on how to pass a Military pilot's course
✈ Life as aircrew in the Military
✈ Your options post Military

Wings has been written by ex-Military flying instructors with a consolidated 50 years experience of learning, flying and teaching. The advice within this book is from those that have been there, done it and taught it.

Various Military Sources

http://www.defencejobs.gov.au/
http://www.defencejobs.gov.au/jobs/aviation.aspx
http://www.airforce.gov.au/
http://www.navy.gov.au/Main_Page
http://www.army.gov.au/
http://www.airforce.com/
http://www.army.mil/
http://www.navy.mil/swf/index.asp
http://www.marines.mil/Pages/Default.aspx
http://www.raf.mod.uk/careers/
http://www.royalnavy.mod.uk/careers
http://www.army.mod.uk/join/26390.aspx

Other Aviation Sources:
http://www.adfmentors.com.au
(Great aptitude training resource including courses and manuals)
http://avfacts.com.au/
(Very useful aviation website, run by the respected Rob Avery.)
http://australianaviation.com.au/
(We are big fans of this magazine. It is great way to stay informed.)